AN INVITATION TO
SOCIAL RESEARCH

Pertti Alasuutari

SAGE Publications
London • Thousand Oaks • New Delhi

First published 1998

SAGE Publications Ltd
6 Bonhill Street
London EC2A 4PU

SAGE Publications Inc
2455 Teller Road
Thousand Oaks, California 91320

SAGE Publications India Pvt Ltd
32, M-Block Market
Greater Kailash – I
New Delhi 110 048

British Library Cataloguing in Publication data

A catalogue record for this book is
available from the British Library.

ISBN 0 7619 5736 7
ISBN 0 7619 5737 5 (pbk)

Library of Congress catalog card number 98–61181

Typeset by Photoprint, Torquay, Devon
Printed in Great Britain by Redwood Books, Trowbridge, Wiltshire

CONTENTS

Preface   ix

1 DETECTIVE STORIES AND SOCIAL RESEARCH   1

2 SOCIOLOGICAL IMAGINATION: WHAT MADE
   IT POSSIBLE?   9
   Administrative apparatus and individualization in society   9
   Knowledge and power   15
   Exchange economy and social research   17
   Detective stories and sociological imagination   19

3 OBSERVATIONS, DEDUCTIONS AND CLUES   25
   Observations and presumptions   25
   Observations and clues   27
   Theoretical framework, method, and model of explanation   28
   From specific to generic, from generic to specific   31
   Clues and evidence   33
   Detective stories, common sense and social research   34

4 THE QUANTIFYING METHOD   39
   Political economy and Marx   41
   Durkheim and statistical analysis   44
   The experimental design   46
   From interview responses to observations   48
   The limits and possibilities of the survey   53
   Explaining differences   58

5 ETHNOGRAPHIC RESEARCH   59

Participant observation   61

Observant participation   66

From the working-class question to youth cultures   72

Towards New Ethnography   75

The presumptions of the ethnographic method   78

6 OBSERVER OR PARTICIPANT?   81

From detective stories to crime novels   81

Critical theory   84

Action research   88

Generally accepted truths as a sociological problem   92

7 STUDYING THE STRUCTURE OF SOCIAL REALITY   97

Language as a closed system   99

Physical and social reality   102

The structure of modern everyday life: a short history   105

Life-style and homological relations   107

The ontology of structure   112

8 FROM THE STUDY OF CULTURAL PRODUCTS TO NARRATIVE ANALYSIS   115

The paradigmatic trend   116

The syntagmatic trend   118

From morphology to mythology   120

Stories and their reception   122

From product analysis to people's own stories   125

From cognitive structures to discourses   127

Method is part of the research setting   128

9 FROM SURVEYS TO IN-DEPTH INTERVIEWS AND CONVERSATIONS   131

From interviews to dialogue as action   131

From informants to respondents   135

In-depth interviews   141

The discursive interview   145

Conversation analysis   152

The end of interviews?   154

10 **DETECTIVE STORIES AND SOCIOLOGICAL
      LITERATURE**   **157**
      Sociology as a force of influence in society   158
      Sociology as a genre of literature   161

References   167

Index   173

PREFACE

The aim of this book is to invite people starting their studies in sociology and other social sciences to the logic of sociological reasoning in an easy-going and entertaining way. How does one study social and cultural phenomena? What is the logic of social research, and what is the difference between qualitative and quantitative analysis? What is the usefulness and sense of studying social phenomena? What is the relationship of socio-logical reasoning to society and to lay thinking? These are the main questions addressed.

To address these questions, I have found it useful to discuss the social origins and evolvement of different forms of the 'sociological imagination'; that is, to introduce their emergence in their social contexts from the classical era all the way to new trends of qualitative methodology. This also enables readers to link up their studies in social research methods with their knowledge of social theory and the history of the social sciences.

Although written with newcomers to the field in mind, this book is more than just a textbook. It presents my own view of social research: how it evolved, where it is going, and what its role is in society. From this perspective, I hope this book is also of interest to other researchers.

To invite new people to the field of social research, I have tried to introduce it in a way that makes it easily approachable, without doing so at the expense of overt simplification. Partly for that reason I have paralleled the historical development of social research with that of detective stories – from eighteenth-century predecessors to Conan Doyle, Christie and the *Black*

Mask school; and from the seventeenth-century Newtonian revolution in science all the way to action research and the linguistic turn.

In my view, the parallel drawn between detective stories and social research is justified at many levels. This book also describes what social research is like by comparing the work of the detective to that of the researcher: how they gather facts, weigh them as clues, and after solving the case present them as evidence. It compares social research to detective stories because the fascination of the latter is based on similar kinds of inferences about social interaction to the former; the only difference is that most people are familiar with detective stories, but have difficulties in transferring this cultural skill to an understanding of sociological analysis. Furthermore, the book contextualizes sociological reasoning by giving an over-all picture of the social history of the sociological imagination. It shows how the two literary genres, i.e. sociological literature and detective stories, stem from the same historical changes in Western civilization.

Although this book is not a methods manual, it gives a general picture of the two methodological approaches known in social sciences: the quantifying method and qualitative analysis. The former was discovered along with the birth of big cities, the division of labour, and the state's need for population statistics, whereas qualitative analysis was discovered along with colonialism and anthropological fieldwork.

This volume is based on my book which initially appeared in 1989 in Finnish as *Erinomaista, rakas Watson: Johdatus yhteiskuntatieteeseen*. At that point the manuscript was read and commented on by Raimo Blom, Risto Heiskala, Lauri Mehtonen, Arto Noro, Keijo Rahkonen and Timo Uusitupa. I want to thank them all for their valuable hints and comments. Now, after quite a few years I was pleased to hear that the book would still be of interest to an international audience. David Silverman wrote a very encouraging review of a summary of the book and the two chapters that David Kivinen and I had already translated. I thought the rest would be a piece of cake, especially because David Kivinen promised to finish the job of translation. However, when setting to work in checking the translation (which is easy when working with David) I realized that times have changed and I have changed with them. Apart

from the (fairly minor) changes due to the international audience I now address instead of only Finnish readers, I realized I
had to update throughout plus add the whole new Chapter 9 to
be able to discuss more recent trends in social research and
social theory. However, I am very pleased with the outcome: I
was able to prepare an updated record of my thinking in this
area, without having to abandon the structure and losing the
fresh feeling of the original manuscript.

Pertti Alasuutari
Tampere

CHAPTER I

DETECTIVE STORIES AND SOCIAL RESEARCH

One of the world's greatest names in detective stories, Sir Arthur Conan Doyle, was born in 1859, the same year that Karl Marx published *A Critique of Political Economy,* a work in which he set out many of the basic tenets for *Capital.* In a sense this critique of Marx's may be regarded as a prelude to the era of classical sociology, which reached maturity around the turn of the century. The late nineteenth century also marks the beginning of the golden age of detective stories: *The Adventures of Sherlock Holmes* was published in 1891, three years before the third volume of *Capital* came out.

By that time, economic upheavals had eroded the traditional social bonds and ways of thinking which held societies together, to the extent that society itself had become visible in a new way, and its structure and inherent causalities came to be seen as a problem. Capitalist development and industrial revolution were a self-evident research object, spiritual father and midwife of the flourishing new science, addressed by all its most important founders – Durkheim, Marx, Simmel, Tönnies, and Weber.

Sherlock Holmes, the world-famous private detective created by Conan Doyle, was concerned in a sense with the self-same mysteries and challenges that originated with the process of social change. The Sherlock Holmes stories were set in a metropolis where the new social division of labour had introduced *Gesellschaft* (societal) relations instead of *Gemeinschaft* (communal) relations (Tönnies), or organic solidarity instead of mechanical solidarity (Durkheim), and where the actions and motives of individuals were least predictable. In this environment the skill of making inferences from the behaviour of perfect strangers was extremely useful. It was this interest that Conan Doyle showed in metropolitan life, its crimes and incidental mysteries, that made his stories so immensely popular. In 'The Adventure of the Blue Carbuncle', for example, Holmes explains to Dr Watson, his friend and great admirer, why he is so interested in an old felt hat:

> No, no. No crime. Only one of those whimsical little incidents which will happen when you have four million human beings all jostling each other within the space of a few square miles. Amid the action and reaction of so dense a swarm of humanity, every possible combination of events may be expected to take place, and many a little problem will be presented which may be striking and bizarre without being criminal. We have already had experience of such.

Conan Doyle's Sherlock Holmes stories were not always about crime; unlike most of his colleagues, Holmes enjoyed the challenge of a difficult problem that would stretch his power of deduction to the very limits. However, taken as a whole, the genre of detective stories was from the outset concerned primarily with solving crimes, and particularly murders.

In this regard, too, detective stories addressed a topical issue. With the collapse of the old social order there was also a gradual dissolution of traditional concepts of morality and law and order, which now became the focus of social and political dispute. Amid the social upheavals, people began to realize that society was not an earthly order created by God, but something that changed and developed with history. True, social development was beyond the influence of any individual, but nevertheless it consisted of ordinary, earthly institutions.

Detective stories took part in the debate on social order by assuring people that justice always prevailed. Sleuths of all descriptions were solving unsolvable crimes and making nonsense of the work of criminal masterminds, convincing the reader that people with opposite interests in society did in fact have important values in common. The subject for detective stories was chosen with this uniting factor in mind: it was understood that decent people, whatever their social views, could never accept murder. Conan Doyle would sometimes let Holmes decide the fate of the criminal, but otherwise, like most writers of the golden age, he had every confidence in the judicial system.

William Godwin (1756–1836), the English political philosopher and originator of the whole genre of crime stories, was on completely different lines in this regard – but it is precisely his dissidence that makes the links between social philosophy and detective stories so clearly visible. Godwin is best known not for his detective stories but for a work entitled *Enquiry Concerning the Principles of Political Justice* (1793), which outlines what he regards as the ideal state of anarchism. Attacking and denouncing various state institutions, including the judicial system, Godwin presents a vision of a world where there is no war, no crime, no so-called administration of law or government. It was very much in the same anarchistic spirit that Godwin one year later published his crime story *The Adventures of Caleb Williams* (1794; originally published under the title *Things as They Are*): his main intention was to prove that the judicial system was corrupt and useless. One of the thieves who appears in his story has this confession to make: 'We who are thieves without a licence, are at open war with another sort of men, who are thieves according to law' (cited in Symons 1992, 36). This was also a central theme in many later detective stories, particularly in the late 1930s and after the Second World War.

One of the main concerns of the literature on detective stories has been to study their concept of science. Asplund (1978) claims that there is a genetic connection between detective stories and the systematic methods of investigation that were developed by early police forces. Both of these, according to Asplund, represent the ideal of positivist research. Asplund refers here to Sherlock Holmes, who was indeed captive to the methods of natural science: Sir Arthur Conan Doyle had a medical education, and his creation adopted a method of deduction (or diagnosis) that was based on the visible traces he found on physical objects.

Carlo Ginzburg (1983), on the other hand, argues that the methods of Sherlock Holmes reflect the theoretical innovations of the late nineteenth century. At that time, scientists began to pay attention to seemingly insignificant observable facts that were thought to provide important clues about the complex reality beneath the visible surface. Ginzburg compares Conan Doyle to two of his contemporaries, the renowned Italian art connoisseur Giovanni Morelli and the father of psychoanalysis, Sigmund Freud. Morelli developed a method for testing the authenticity of paintings, which was based on the minutest examination of unnoticeable, insignificant details. He said that it is easiest to detect a forger by looking at such details in which it is hardest to copy the style of the master: in the strokes of the brush, or in the shape of ears and hands. The artist's personality is most clearly visible in these small details. Freud's method and theory of personality is based on this very same idea: his focus is on dreams, slips of the tongue, etc. Holmes, too, bases his conclusions on minute traces: he makes assumptions about what has caused those traces, and then constructs in his mind's eye a train of events which explains each and every visible piece of evidence.

These interpretations by Asplund and Ginzburg are both justified and do not even conflict with each other. Conan Doyle's stories of Sherlock Holmes are so rich in detail that it is impossible to slot the detective's methods into any single category of theoretical approach. On the other hand, these stories represent only the beginning of a whole genre in which we can find examples of virtually all schools and perspectives of social research and social philosophy.

The purpose of this book is not to offer an interpretation of Holmes and other detective stories; I do not aim to explain how detective stories should be read and understood. Rather, detective stories serve as examples, providing insights into how times have changed, how our ways of thinking have changed. Detective stories originate with the Industrial Revolution and the urban way of life. They have become more and more psychological, reflecting the tendencies in Western society towards individualization. The choice of subject in detective stories, their characters and how these have changed, all reflect real changes in society.

Detective stories also capture the spirit and atmosphere of the times in which they were written. This is important because the present book is concerned to examine social research and the kinds of methods it has applied as products of the era in which they were devised. There are obviously other and better ways of describing the atmosphere of a certain era than by means of a few impressionistic excerpts from detective stories. However, for the present purposes detective stories are particularly relevant: they, too, are concerned with research work, with the application of different research methods, and with the drawing of conclusions from given evidence. Detective stories can tell us a great deal about how people in a certain age drew inferences from human activity and from social relationships. They can help us tie down the methods of social science to their respective historical contexts.

We are inclined to examine phenomena or ways of thinking as products of a certain era only once that era has passed. In this sense 'historical' is seen as synonymous with 'incorrect'. If a research method is to give a truthful picture of social reality, then it is held that that method must be valid and applicable to any historical era. The view advocated in this book is different. Sociological research has its own specific conditions out of which it has grown, and also its own specific research methods. These are historical, in at least two senses. Firstly, changes in the object of study make it possible to develop new kinds of methods. For example, statistical social research began to gather momentum when official statistics became available. Secondly, the methods and ways of describing and analysing the object of social research tend to shape that object according to the model that is applied in the description and analysis. Consider, for instance, psychological theories which explain crime by reference to traumas experienced in early childhood. Regardless of whether these theories are true or not, they are still part of social reality; and they are actually used when people try to explain and interpret their own and each other's behaviour. Similarly, sociological research produces different kinds of categories and classifications that people use in defining themselves and constructing their identity. Sometimes sociologists make predictions about the future, and responses by different parties to social policy mean that those predictions have at least some impact on the real course of development, no matter how 'wrong' the predictions were. So in many respects the methods of social research, its descriptions and results are neither right nor wrong. Social research is quite simply an integral part of modern society. Its methods change with history, together with its objects of study.

In this book the weight is, in other words, on the methodological questions of social research. Of course, methods cannot
be discussed in isolation from social theories because researchers always look at their object of study within a given theoretical framework. The choice of method is very much dependent
on each researcher's views on social reality and its nature.
However, an introduction to all the major social theories is
beyond the scope of this book. The discussion moves in the
middle ground between theories and methods, which is called
methodology.

Detective stories provide excellent lessons in research
methods. The sheer ingenuity and clarity of much of the advice
that Sherlock Holmes gives to Dr Watson, for instance, easily
stands comparison with the wisdom of textbooks on research
methods. However, as was already implied above, the purpose
here is not to compare Conan Doyle or any other detective-story
writer to the great philosophers or methodologists. With all due
respect, Conan Doyle is simply not worthy of such a comparison; or should I say that his merits would not be fully
appreciated in this company. The same applies in fact to all
creations of detective-story writers, no matter how fascinating
and ingenious their ideas. Detective stories merely provide
examples of the application, in everyday contexts, of the human
capacity of logical reasoning – even though those examples are
almost always out of an imaginary world and sometimes even
untrue, and far removed from the real world in which the
readers live out their everyday lives. Nonetheless the plot of the
story, the means that the leading character uses to dig out clues,
the solution of the crime, are based on facts that *could*, in
principle, happen; indeed the reader who pays careful attention
to all the details could in most cases resolve the mystery by
correctly interpreting the given clues, just as the character in the
book is doing.

The 'democratic' structure of detective stories does not teach
the reader how to draw the 'right' conclusions. The attraction of
detective stories lies precisely in the ability of the reader to
piece together the clues and on this basis to make logical
inferences. Of course a detective-story writer may try to mislead
the reader by intentionally withholding vital clues so that, in
the end, the solution comes as a surprise, even to the most
careful reader. If the reader solves the problem before the

detective, the story will lose all interest. All the same, the main attraction of detective stories is based on the readership's existing conceptions about solving mysteries; on the readership's sociological imagination.

By 'sociological imagination' I mean the making of rational inferences from mysteries that are related to human activity and human interaction. Human activity, interaction and the various institutions of social life are studied by many different disciplines, not only sociology, and therefore the discussion below is also not restricted to the work and to the methods that are applied in sociology departments. However, I find the term itself – which comes from the title of an excellent book by C. Wright Mills (1977) too appropriate not to use it. The same applies to the use of the word 'sociology' throughout the book: for example, when I speak in Chapter 10 of sociological literature, I am referring to all publications that deal with social and societal phenomena.

In this broad sense, then, sociological imagination is not an asset on which sociologists have a monopoly. This book discusses the general methical and methodological principles of social research, turning occasionally to detective stories in search of examples, and from this vantage-point aims to conceptualize the methods and procedures that we all use in our everyday lives – or at least when we are reading detective stories.

In this regard this book does not really add anything new to our existing knowledge of the world. A conceptual discussion of these methods and procedures merely makes possible the *application* of sociological imagination to social research. The chapters of this book are accordingly introductions to the methods that social research has used in attempting to analyse human activity, interaction and social institutions. In spite of its many distinctive characteristics sociological research does not differ in qualitative terms from the chains of deduction that are familiar to us from detective stories. Both grow up out of the sociological imagination that was aroused in the intelligentsia as well as in ordinary people with the breakthrough of capitalism. It is only that of the two genres dealing with sociological imagination, detective stories are much more widely known than sociological literature.

CHAPTER 2

SOCIOLOGICAL IMAGINATION: WHAT MADE IT POSSIBLE?

There are three themes that are directly relevant to the growth of sociological imagination, to the question of what made it possible: the development of official statistics, the growing importance of monetary economy, and the evolution of modern urban society. Although these themes are obviously closely interwoven, a closer analysis exposes two different periods. The earlier period, in the sixteenth and seventeenth centuries, gave rise to the object of social research, i.e. 'society', and it also saw the first empirical studies that were concerned with it. The second period, from the early nineteenth century to the beginning of the twentieth century, saw the masses take a growing interest in rational deduction concerning human behaviour and interpersonal relationships.

Administrative apparatus and individualization in society

Empirical social research started at around the same time as the Newtonian–Galilean revolution in the natural sciences, i.e. in the late seventeenth century.[1] In both cases the new ways of

---

1. Isaac Newton's *Philosophiae Naturalis Principia Mathematica*, widely acknowledged as a major milestone in this revolution, was published in 1687. Empirical, quantitative social research is accordingly dated at 1662. From this

thinking implied the application of mathematical models to empirical phenomena. Prior to the seventeenth century, mathematics was used exclusively by astronomers, but from then on it was also applied to study the 'world under the moon', i.e. society and other natural phenomena occurring on earth – phenomena which, according to the Aristotelian, dualistic world-view, did not observe the same laws as the 'world above the moon'. So it was not that social research borrowed its model from the natural sciences; the turning-points came more or less simultaneously in both fields. Indeed, there were many scholars who were interested in studying both social and natural phenomena. In the search for explanations it is necessary to turn instead to the changes taking place in the Western way of life and world-view, changes that gave rise to 'society', the object of quantitative and empirical social research.

The notion of 'society' was introduced into the European languages in the sixteenth century. In English the word 'society', which previously referred to a sense of companionship, began to be used as the general term for the body of institutions and relationships within which a large group of people live. In the eighteenth century it acquired a more abstract second sense as the condition in which such institutions and relationships are formed (Williams 1988, 291–295). Although society refers to a complex, invisible system, it is considered a very real, concrete fact. It is said that although society is composed of individuals, there nevertheless applies a given set of laws; that society is more than the sum total of its constituent parts (Trilling 1971, 19).

The history of a word is not necessarily contemporaneous with the history of the thought-model that the word gave a name. However, historians of European culture are more or less agreed that people's ways of thinking changed quite dramatically in the late sixteenth and early seventeenth centuries. In his studies of human civilization Norbert Elias (1978, 1982) observes that manners began rapidly to change from the sixteenth century onwards, both in courts and among ordinary

---

perspective the notion that the beginning of the natural sciences and human sciences date from different points is false. The thesis is the same if the beginning of scientific research is set at the Aristotelian science system in which every major natural science and human science has its early beginnings. Further, classical French and English political economy is at least as old as certain major fields of natural scientific research at this time.

people, so that table manners, for instance, corresponded (among the upper classes) to present-day manners by the end of the eighteenth century. From there on it was mainly a matter of customs spreading and establishing themselves. The same applies to the history of sexuality: the period of modesty, silence and increasing prohibitions is usually said to have dawned in the early seventeenth century (e.g. Foucault 1978). According to Frances Yates (1969), the early part of the seventeenth century was an important period for the birth of modern European and American personhood.

The birth of the 'individual' also implied the birth of 'society'. It was not until people began to see themselves as separate from others that they could begin to conceive of 'society' as a system or organism consisting of 'individuals', yet observing its own laws. The experience among individuals of the existence of a 'society' gave rise to the idea that those individuals could be ruled on the strength of a closer familiarity with those laws.

To govern a group of people, to control their affairs, it was necessary to have information, and it was to meet this need that official statistics were introduced in the sixteenth and seventeenth centuries in Europe. In England, for instance, specific mortality tables were compiled on the basis of parish registers as early as 1563 (Bernal 1971, 1048). These tables are significant in the sense that one of the first ever empirical social studies, *Natural and Political Observations Made Upon the Bills of Mortality* by John Graunt in 1662, was based on a statistical analysis of these tables. Another important work was published that same year, William Petty's *A Treatise of Taxes and Contributions*. Indeed 1662 is generally considered to mark the beginning of empirical, quantitative social research.

This was not the first time in recorded history that information was collected on the population and its wealth for purposes of administration. The first attempt at a geographical description and census of the population was made in China way back in 2238 BC, and it is possible that a population census was taken in Egypt around 3600–3500 BC. It is known for sure that a census was completed in Egypt in 1700–1600 BC. In England, the early history of surveys dates back to 1086, when William the Conqueror commissioned Domesday Book, a survey of the population, the acreage of arable land and other property in the counties under his rule.

However, empirical social research is thought to have started with the studies by Graunt and Petty: these were the first two works that used the data they collected as a vantage-point for systematic argumentation. This was in marked contrast to earlier work which consisted simply in the collection of statistical data, without any attempt to make any deductions or generalizations from the numbers. For instance, the 'results' of Domesday Book were not presented even in tabular form, but the numerical evidence on each 'observation unit' (i.e. county) was presented in the text describing each county.

The situation was entirely different in the case of Graunt and Petty. On the basis of his analyses of causes of death and birth rate statistics, John Graunt demonstrated that the frequency of certain causes of death showed a constant statistical association with total mortality, that mortality was higher in urban areas than in rural areas, that although boys outnumbered girls among newborn babies the total number of men and women in the population remained more or less the same, and that mortality was high in the first years of life. William Petty, for his part, is regarded as the intellectual father of the new research method, although there has been much disagreement about his influence on Graunt's study (indeed about whether he actually contributed in the capacity of author). William Petty, a doctor, natural philosopher and economist, forcefully advocated the use of numerical data in resolving all sorts of practical and political problems. He called this new discipline *political arithmetic*.

The 'political' in this new discipline referred specifically to government and to administration. According to Charles Davenant (1656–1712), one of the representatives of the new branch of science, political arithmetic refers to numeric reasoning dealing with government.

However, empirical social research was not just a response to needs for more efficient government, nor was it just a by-product of the development of official statistics; it was also and importantly an indication of a profound change in the style or mode of government. In antiquity and during the Middle Ages order was maintained by public demonstrations of the repressive apparatus and its power to rule and to punish criminals, llowing law-abiding citizens to remain in the background and e their lives in peace. But from the eighteenth century

onwards power and the centres of power became increasingly invisible, while citizens became targets of continuous and visible surveillance and control. This is also reflected in architecture: in antiquity there were temples, theatres and circuses, whereas the modern age is characterized by architectonic solutions based on the principle of the Panopticon (Foucault 1979, 216).

The Panopticon is an architectural design specifically intended for surveillance purposes. It consists of a circular structure divided into cells, each facing a central tower. There are two windows in each cell, one facing towards the central tower and one facing the opposite direction, allowing light to pass through the cell. It follows that the guard stationed in the central tower can see into each cell, but the inmate in the cell cannot see the centralized supervisor. According to English philosopher Jeremy Bentham (1748–1832), who invented the Panopticon, this spatial arrangement allows for close surveillance of the insane, patients, inmates, workers or schoolchildren as individuals; the inmates in their cells can see neither each other nor their supervisor, but they are nonetheless constantly aware that they are visible and under surveillance – regardless of whether there is anyone there actually observing them.

The Panopticon produces an impersonal power relationship in which the object of surveillance is individualized. The reason why this relationship has such tremendous impact lies in the subject's awareness of the possibility of continuous surveillance, which inevitably influences his or her behaviour and which consequently makes the subject a carrier of this relationship. The unfolding network of power relations is independent of the observer's motives in each case.

The growth and development of the modern individual and modern society meant that 'panopticism' became the all-pervasive principle of social order and power relations. The threat of chaos and disorder that lay dormant in the faceless crowds of modern society was countered by means of systematic surveillance, control and data collection on individuals.

Initially this method was applied in the late seventeenth century to combat the chaos that was created in urban areas by the plague. Houses were boarded up and closed from the outside, all public meetings and gatherings were prohibited, and guards were placed everywhere, at all gates and in every quarter. The same means were employed in eighteenth-century Paris to combat social unrest and crime. An invisible network of intense surveillance consisting of police inspectors, observers, police informers and prostitutes was set up, its job to lay bare, to make everything visible (Foucault 1979).

There was a growing sense of resentment among the Parisian populace at the continuing expansion of surveillance and control, in spite of its invisibility. The masses who lived in the city and who provided a useful hiding place and cover for criminals and anyone else came under the ruthless, all-revealing spotlight of the panoptic apparatus. In 1836 Balzac wrote the following lines in *Modeste Mignon*:

> Poor women of France! You would probably like to remain unknown in order to carry on your little romances. But how can you manage to do this in a civilization which registers the departure and arrival of coaches in public places, counts letters and stamps them when they are posted and again when they are delivered, which provides houses with numbers and will soon have the whole country to the smallest plot of land in its registers?

The surveillance also gave rise to some resistance. The working class, for example, was opposed to the numbering of houses, which Napoleon's administration had made obligatory in 1805. As late as 1864 the carpenters who lived in the Saint-Antoine section of Paris continued to give their address in the form of the name of their house rather than its number. In the long run this was of course all in vain. The complex web of registers and different forms of surveillance meant it was impossible for people to disappear in the masses without leaving some trace of themselves (Benjamin 1973, 47).

Modern society also saw a movement away from the brutal, public means of punishment that were favoured in the Middle Ages towards more humane forms of imprisonment and towards closed institutions that were committed to the ideals of moral education. However, as Walter Benjamin and Foucault have shown, this has not necessarily translated into progress. The new system is one of relentless, all-embracing surveillance and control which leaves no one untouched, not even the most law-abiding of citizens. The key thing about the change, however, was not that people were subjected to non-stop surveillance. Rather, it is our awareness of the ever-present existence of the administrative apparatus, our knowledge that the system can intervene at any time and at any place, our anticipation of the embarrassing consequences of such an intervention, that keeps us on the straight and narrow path. External discipline and overt coercion have largely been replaced by self-discipline. In this process of civilization, the general mentality of the modern individual has changed quite considerably. The growth of self-discipline at the expense of external discipline over the past few centuries has made the latter more and more redundant and contributed to a growing sense of freedom among individuals. In this sense, as far as people's own experiences are concerned, modernization has implied a growth of *freedom*. It is not that people today feel they are *subjecting* themselves, against their own will, to imposed order and discipline, but they *take into account* the social coercions which set the conditions for their voluntary actions. For the most part the advanced form of social order becomes a natural environment, the activity it expects of people becomes *consistent with one's own will*. These variable conditions, which seem to appear all by themselves and which no longer represent the personal power of the ruler or the coercive apparatus, are now perceived as representing a mystical 'society' that is opposed to the individual.

Knowledge and power

The seeds of sociological imagination were sown with these changes in living conditions and mentality. The surveillance and control apparatus provided a useful model for socio-technological research and often the materials it needed to boot.

The task of identifying the individual within the faceless masses and monitoring the individual's actions was a job for the organized police service. It created an entirely new line of inquiry, criminal technology, whose most famous pioneer was Frenchman Alphonse Bertillon (1853–1914). Bertillon developed what was known as the anthropometric method of identifying criminals, which was used for compiling data into criminal records prior to the introduction of the fingerprint method. Bertillon's innovation and great personal skill in resolving crimes made him world-famous. However, he was very much a product of his time. It was not until the birth of the large city following the Industrial Revolution that there was any point or any need to identify individuals using exact methods of measurement. In rural society, everyone knew each other in any case (Asplund 1978). Quantitative social research applied the same model and method that was familiar from the Panopticon: identification and surveillance allows for an experimental design, as Bentham had pointed out. The Panopticon can also, Bentham continued, be used as a laboratory for scientific experiments, for changing the behaviour of those under observation, and for disciplining and punishing individuals.

According to Foucault, the modern disciplines that are concerned with human nature and human behaviour grew up out of this panoptic power structure of modern society. During the eighteenth century, surveillance systems and power structures became more and more closely interwoven so that eventually the accumulation of knowledge and the growth of power had a mutually reinforcing effect on one another. The expansion of the panoptic order and its application to new institutions – hospitals, schools, workshops – gave rise to corresponding branches of knowledge and research for each institution: for instance, clinical medicine, psychiatry, child psychology, educational psychology and the rationalization of labour use (Foucault 1979, 224).

Foucault argues that forms of knowledge always correspond to forms of power. This entails the radical idea that disciplinary practices, such as Panopticism, produce corresponding fields of knowledge, or disciplines. Vice versa, a new form of knowledge implies a change in the prevailing power relations. Thus knowledge in itself, in terms of both its form and content, is one party in the struggle and debate waged over the direction of social development. Knowledge consists not only of observations of an outside object, such as the entity known as 'society', but the acquisition and application of knowledge is in itself a societal practice. Knowledge and power, up to a certain point, are synonymous.

Any 'fact' or thought-model put forward by an individual can always be examined as a construct that has evolved under a given set of social circumstances, as reflecting the meanings generated by those circumstances and as commentary on those circumstances. It is not easy for the social sciences to find eternal truths or universally valid laws because their object of study – 'society' – is not an entity independent of the researcher in the same way as the object of the natural sciences. The acquisition and application of knowledge concerning social phenomena are in themselves social practices, an integral part of the complex of activities that we call society. Social research is one way of trying to influence and change things in society.

Exchange economy and social research

The growth and development of empirical social research was also very much influenced by the increasing significance of a monetary exchange economy and the subsequent breakthrough of capitalism. There are three relevant dimensions here. Firstly, the growth of monetary exchange meant that people became more and more dependent for their income on a growing number of other people. It was indeed largely through money and monetary exchange relations that people perceived this system of mutual dependencies that was known as 'society'. Secondly, the logic of monetary exchange relations was a tough, merciless school of individualism. It taught people to defend their own best interests and to look upon the other party to the exchange relationship as an opponent. Thirdly, the exchange economy represented the network of interpersonal relationships in numeric form, so the most logical way to investigate the secrets of that network was by means of modern mathematical models.

It is understandable, therefore, that when the era of political arithmetic began to fade, the attentions of empirical social research were very much focused on the economy of capitalist society. Originating in the eighteenth century, this line of inquiry is known as political economy. Its so-called classical period is marked by the work of Adam Smith (1723–1790) and David Ricardo (1772–1823), and it culminated in the theories of Karl Marx (1818–1883). After Marx, economics developed into a separate discipline that was concerned to find optimal strategies of economic activity.

William Petty's study on taxation may be regarded as the first work in this line of research (Bernal 1971, 1049). Petty focused exclusively on the 'language of economy', on measures, figures and weights. This is how Petty described his methodological approach in the *Political Arithmetick*, written in 1676:

> Instead of using only comparative and superlative words, and intellectual Arguments, I have taken the course (as a Specimen of the Political Arithmetick I have long aimed at) to express my self in terms of *Number, Weight*, or *Measure*; to use only arguments of Sense, and to consider only such Causes, as have visible Foundations in Nature; leaving those that depend upon mutable Minds, Opinions, Appetites, and Passions of particular Men, to the consideration of others. (Petty 1963, 244)

Political economy developed at a time when the masses living in cities and monetary exchange relations between individuals were still a novel, strange phenomenon. Benjamin (1973, 62–63) has the following description:

> For the crowd really is the spectacle of nature – if one may apply the term to social conditions. A street, a conflagration, or a traffic accident assemble people who are not defined along class lines. They present themselves as concrete gatherings, but socially they remain abstract – namely, in their isolated private interests. Their models are the customers who, each in his private interest, gather at the market around their 'common cause'. In many cases, such gatherings have only a statistical existence. This existence conceals the really monstrous thing about them: the concentration of private persons as such by the accident of their private interests.

In the modern city it is quite clear and apparent that the people living there are no longer necessarily a coherent community with shared rules and a good mutual understanding. On the contrary, communities have more in common with natural phenomena: they are like a pile of sand-grains washed down with the stream along the mountainside, or like scurrying ants in a huge anthill. It may be possible to predict the numbers and the movements of individuals in groups of people if one knows what causes their movement.

Concealed within this system of individual and group movements there seemed to lie a simple yet secret order. Just as a patient examination of an anthill will reveal that each and every ant has a specific task to complete, the movements of most individuals in cities are explained by what they are doing to earn an income: going to work to the factory, shop or office, finding their way to the shopping centre to buy food, returning home for the night. This explains a great deal of what one sees in the street: from what people are wearing it is possible to deduce how much money they have and often what sort of job they have (because the two are closely related), the direction in which they are heading and their mode of transport indicates (primarily) either where they live or where they work, but indirectly many other inferences can also be drawn. In other words, the examination of 'measures, figures and weights' seemed to explain most of what was worth knowing. Mathematics and statistics presented themselves as the best conceivable methodology because much of social reality had already been translated into numbers – in the form of price tags in shops and wage statistics, for instance.

Detective stories and sociological imagination

The nineteenth century was a significant turning-point in social thought and research. Empirical social research and official statistics expanded and were institutionalized. Reformist doctors and philanthropists in France started to do statistical social research, and in England statistical societies were set up in the 1830s to try to resolve the labour question. By the middle of the nineteenth century, statistical social research took important steps towards greater methodological uniformity when Adolphe Quételet (1796–1874) in Belgium published several articles on 'moral-statistical' research, some of them in French and English journals (Lazarsfeld 1961). Frenchman Frédéric Le Play (1806–1882) also had a significant role: he collected materials for a study on family types from several European countries (Goldfrank 1972). As the reputation of Quetelet and Le Play began to spread across Europe, their methods of statistical research were also widely adopted.

The middle of the nineteenth century was also an important period in the sense that ordinary people began to show a growing interest in making, and growing need to make, rational inferences about interindividual relationships and the essence of different character types. Indirectly, this is evidenced by the growth of the genre of detective stories and its great popularity among people in the cities. The need to draw conclusions about human activity is a specifically urban phenomenon. Walter Benjamin neatly captures this trend among Parisians in his essay 'The Flâneur' (1973, 35–36).

In the early decades of the nineteenth century, Benjamin tells us, Parisians favoured a specific type of light reading: the pocket-sized paperbacks sold out on the streets of Paris were known as *physiologies*. Physiologies detailed different character types that anyone could see and meet simply by observing the crowds at marketplaces. There was hardly a character in Paris of whom a physiology had not been compiled: everyone was covered from the petty traders and hucksters along the boulevards to sherry-sipping dandies in the foyers of the opera-house. When all these characters had been exhausted, physiologies turned to the places and sites of Paris; then to nations; and eventually to animals. The best year for physiologies was 1841, when a total of 76 new titles were published. Popular interest then began to wane and by the late 1940s the genre had disappeared from the market altogether. Physiologies were now replaced by a new genre of mass entertainment: the detective story.

According to Benjamin, both detective stories and physiologies corresponded to the life-situation and way of life produced by the large city: the situation in which, for the first time in recorded history, large masses of people had to rely on their eyesight to cope in everyday life. With the development of public transport in the form of railways and trams, people had to learn to spend minutes or even hours on end watching each other without being able to speak to one another. This was a frightening situation: you could never tell what sort of criminals you might be facing, whatever their profession or social class. Early physiologies tried to reassure their readership by saying that any and all of the groups of people whom they, the educated classes, were likely to come across, such as members of the working class, were completely harmless and friendly. However, these reassurances did not work for very long because in their everyday life, people were to encounter each other in the capacity of debtor and creditor, buyer and seller, employer and employee – in a word as rivals. Therefore physiologies began to assure people that anyone with a keen eye for detail can easily deduce the occupation, character, background and life-style of most passers-by.

The observation and analysis of fellow humans and urban life and the drawing of inferences from those observations was not restricted to the pages of physiologies and detective stories. Increasingly, intellectuals and the bourgeoisie in cities took a practical interest in making such inferences. According to Benjamin (1973, 39), Delvau, an artist friend of Baudelaire's, said it was just as easy for him to slot the people of Paris into different categories as it was for the geologist to distinguish between different rock layers.

The growing interest in deduction from everyday life goes some way towards explaining the growth and immense popularity of the new genre that grew up out of physiologies, i.e. detective stories. Edgar Allan Poe, whose detective stories were devoured by Parisians from the 1840s onwards, apparently shared the same view: 'I do not mean to say that they are not ingenious – but people think them more ingenious than they are – on account of their method and air of method' (cited in Symons 1992, 47).

The publication in England in 1887 of the first Sherlock Holmes story, 'A Study in Scarlet', met with an even more enthusiastic response. With the exception of the Bible, there exist no other works that have been published in as many different languages and in as many editions as the stories of Sherlock Holmes. In the late nineteenth-century, people in Britain were absolutely fascinated by the skill with which Holmes made his deductions from such trivial details as a seedy hard-felt hat, as in 'The Adventure of the Blue Carbuncle':

> That the man was highly intellectual is of course obvious upon the face of it, and also that he was fairly well-to-do within the last three years, although he has now fallen upon evil days. He had foresight, but has less now than formerly, pointing to a moral retrogression, which, when taken with the decline of his fortunes, seems to indicate some evil influence, probably drink, at work upon him. This may account also for the obvious fact that his wife has ceased to love him.

What exactly was the appeal of these kinds of inferences to Arthur Conan Doyle's contemporaries and to subsequent generations? The literature has drawn attention to the fact that the aim of the leading characters in detective stories and in the emerging art of criminal technology was to set apart the individual from others, to identify the physical or psychological characteristics of this individual. Asplund (1978) points out that Alphonse Bertillon, who developed the anthropometric method for identifying criminals, was a contemporary of Conan Doyle's and known to him. Asplund goes on to draw a parallel from criminal technology and detective stories to behaviourist psychology and positivist social science, which date from around the same period. In behaviourism, the individual is identified from a series of numeric values based on individual measurement results; and the plot in detective stories from the golden age also revolved around the identification of the murderer from a limited number of suspects.

There can be no doubt that the development of the modern, individually centred society contributed to the growth of both detective stories and sociological imagination. The link, however, as far as I can see, is an indirect one: the object of deduction, whether in everyday urban life or in detective stories, is not to identify individuals but to *classify* and in this way to gain valuable clues for further inferences about different trains of events. The nineteenth-century discovery which appealed to so many readers, that it was possible from the marks on a hat to make far-reaching conclusions about the owner's life history, was in effect based on the observation of how similar modern individuals are to one another; how similar their thought-patterns, motives and fates; and how narrow the range of social types from which to pick a model that matches the person in question.

The impact of this discovery was evident in both social research and detective stories. For instance, the motives for murders in detective stories of the golden age are almost always the same: revenge, jealousy, personal gain or protecting a position achieved. Accordingly, the only assumption made about human subjects in political economy was that of individuals pursuing their own personal interest.

In a word, by the nineteenth century the structures and subjects of modern society had established themselves to such an extent that what at first glance appeared as a wholly chaotic social life was in fact a controllable system both in practical and conceptual terms. During this period a framework and language emerged with which people were to talk about society and the groups of people and phenomena belonging to that society; in Britain, for instance, the concept of 'class' was adopted in common usage (Williams 1982).

CHAPTER 3

OBSERVATIONS, DEDUCTIONS AND CLUES

Observations and presumptions

Everything we know and everything we believe about the world is based on observations and inferences drawn from those observations. Observations consist of any information we receive: what we see, feel, taste, hear from others or read about in books.

It may be tempting to assume that the observations which make up the material for empirical research are somehow different from other, everyday observations: that they are 'experiential' or 'first-hand information' – that scientific knowledge is not based on hearsay. There are, however, no grounds for such a distinction. The material used in linguistics and in many surveys in the social sciences, for example, consists of ordinary, everyday talk. Interview statements, books, TV programmes, other studies, in a word any material may provide the primary data that are considered the hallmark of empirical research. In the end it all depends on the research problem and on the point of view from which the observations are examined.

Even the simplest of observations can never be 'pure', stripped of all presumptions, as Peirce (cited in Sebeok and Umiker-Sebeok 1983, 16) points out:

> Looking out my window this lovely spring morning I see an azalea in full bloom. No, no! I do not see that; though that is the only way

I can describe what I see. *That* is a proposition, a sentence, a fact; but what I perceive is not proposition, sentence, fact, but only an image, which I can make intelligible in part by means of a statement of fact. This statement is abstract, but what I see is concrete. I perform an abduction when I so much as express in a sentence anything I see. The truth is that the whole fabric of our knowledge is one matted felt of pure hypothesis confirmed and refined by induction. Not the smallest advance can be made in knowledge beyond the stage of vacant staring, without making an abduction at every step.

No matter how simple and straightforward the observation, it contains a whole world-history, a conception that has been passed on through generations as to what matters in the world and how its different elements are named. No one can stand apart and remain unaffected by all the *presumptions* that have accumulated from one generation to the next and that structure perceptions of the world. The collection and interpretation of different kinds of information about nature, society and human activity is always based on an underlying set of given, existing assumptions about the nature of reality. There do not exist pure, unconditional facts, but observations are always theory-laden. A fresh view of something that is considered self-evident, say of something that did *not* happen, requires of the researcher a critical examination of his or her presumptions as well as new, innovative ways of combining those premises with new observations – as is illustrated by the following excerpt from Conan Doyle's story 'Silver Blaze':

'Is there any point to which you would wish to draw my attention?'
    'To the curious incident of the dog in the night-time.'
    'The dog did nothing in the night-time.'
    'That was the curious incident,' remarked Sherlock Holmes.

Holmes focused his attention on the fact that the dog did not bark, even though someone had entered the stables it was supposed to be guarding, and stolen a horse. This observation was based on the common, existing presumption that the dog would have barked had the thief been someone the dog did not know.

Observations and clues

In the process of inference that aims at resolving a certain problem, observations are not taken simply as they come, at face-value, as they would normally be. Instead, they are actively produced either by analysing one's observations or by making new ones from a different angle or by different means. Observations are analysed into their constituent parts, which are then examined in a critical light against one's presumptions about the world. Nor are observations, old or new, regarded as 'discoveries'; they are taken as *clues*, as indications of features or dimensions of reality that may not be immediately apparent to the observer.

The detection of new clues is not necessarily dependent on the sharpness of one's senses or the accuracy of the technical means applied. Technical means (such as a magnifying glass) can of course help to uncover small details that are not visible to the naked eye – but even the best equipment cannot make up for the skill of combining new observations and presumptions in fresh, creative, surprising ways.

Sherlock Holmes is quite unrivalled in his sense for detail and perceptive observation. He never tires of teaching his method to his apprentice and admirer Dr Watson. He takes every possible opportunity to apply his skill of deduction, often just to show off or to amuse himself. So when Dr Watson enters the room with a whiff of iodoform, his index finger blotched with a stain from a cone of lunar caustic, and his hat dented where he would hide his stethoscope, Holmes infers that his friend must have taken up his medical practice again.

This example makes clear the difference between an observation and a clue. A keen eye can detect a dent in a hat or a stain on an index finger; a keen nose can detect the scent of iodoform. However, it requires the power of deduction to infer that the dent in the hat may have been caused by a stethoscope, that a stain on the finger is explained by the use of a cone of lunar caustic, and that the scent of iodoform is associated with medical practice. Taken separately, each of these assumptions is doubtful, just one possible explanation of many; but taken together, they provide a strong indication to Sherlock Holmes that Dr Watson has been practising his profession again.

Theoretical framework, method, and model of explanation

For each observation the researcher must also consider whether it is a relevant clue in this particular case: is it part of the chain of events that is under investigation? All sorts of strange things happen in life, but not all of them are necessarily connected. In Raymond Chandler's *The Lady in the Lake*, Philip Marlowe is looking for a woman who has gone missing. Since her disappearance the woman had been seen in a hotel in the company of a man called Lavery. Marlowe goes to visit this man but finds him murdered. He learns about a mountain chalet, which he visits, and there he finds the caretaker's wife drowned. Marlowe describes these events to a police officer, who is confused:

> 'Why are you telling me this? Are you implying a connexion?'
> 'There's a connexion in time. Lavery had been up there. I don't know of any other connexion, but I thought I'd better mention it.'

It is up to the investigator to decide which observations are relevant to resolving the case. To this end the investigator will need to have a basic hunch or assumption about an entity that in detective stories is known as a 'case'. For purposes of data collection, hunches or preliminary assumptions are needed about the 'extent' of that case.

Social research has to go through these same basic steps to demarcate its research problems. Decisions have to be taken as to the extent of the questions that will be addressed and how they will be addressed because no single study can provide an answer to all conceivable questions. On the other hand, it is important that the researcher does not exclude observations which would appear to be relevant to the problem or 'case' in hand – at least not without explaining the reason for this omission.

The kind of observations that the researcher makes and the decision as to which of those observations are relevant will depend on both the theoretical framework and the research method adopted. The method must be compatible with the theoretical framework, but it must also have an independence all its own.

The *research method* consists of the practices and operations with which the researcher produces observations. Consider Sherlock Holmes: in the search for clues Holmes concentrates on the physical traces of the chain of events rather than trying to find out what sort of characters were involved by interviewing people or intervening in the course of events. Holmes depends on his magnifying glass rather than advanced interview techniques or routine footwork, which was to become the trademark of so many later detectives. Holmes does of course interview his clients to find out what has happened, but he does not use the interview material for analytical purposes to the same extent as Agatha Christie's characters, for instance, who want to try to look 'behind' people's reactions and statements.

The tactic of Miss Marple, one of Agatha Christie's famous characters, is to ask surprising questions or to make seemingly dumb comments and then to closely observe the reactions among the people who are present. The focal concern is not with the explicit response or with the truth-value of the 'testimony'; instead this 'interview method' is concerned to see what sort of inferences can be made from this or that reaction to the investigator's provocation. Another Christie character, the Belgian detective Hercule Poirot, draws on his famous power of reasoning but also pays close attention to the intuitive comments and observations made by the people involved in the case. On the last pages of *Hercule Poirot's Christmas*, for instance, Poirot says that the two most important keys to resolving the mystery came in the inadvertent comments by two different persons:

> The first was when Mrs Alfred Lee quoted a line from *Macbeth*: *'Who would have thought the old man to have had so much blood in him?'* The other was a phrase uttered by Tressilian, the butler. He described how he felt dazed and things seemed to be happening that had happened before.

The first comment helped Poirot reach the conclusion that animal blood, mixed with sodium citrate to prevent coagulation, had been added to the scene of the murder. The butler's feeling that it had all happened before was explained by the fact that in addition to the murdered son of the old man he had two other illegitimate sons living in the house, all three resembling one another. This method can be compared to the research approach that Harré and Secord (1972) call *ethogenics*, in which people are regarded not as passive objects of observation but as active subjects with their own interpretations of things.

The researcher's decision as to what amount to relevant observations to the case, what sort of observations are worth collecting and producing, will depend upon the range of explanations that are considered feasible in that particular case. This range of possible solutions could be described as the study's underlying *theoretical framework*. For example, the theoretical framework in detective stories of the golden age consists of the most typical motives for murder: the detective's assumption is that the murderer's motive was either revenge, jealousy, personal interest or madness. As for the various events related to the case, the theoretical framework is that there must be a rational explanation even for the most curious of events. In Arthur Conan Doyle's *The Hound of the Baskervilles*, for instance, Sherlock Holmes did not believe for a minute that the Baskerville family had been haunted from generation to generation by the same devilish dog. This sort of theoretical framework, in the context of detective stories, means that the search for clues is restricted to the motives of the people involved and, on the other hand, to the chains of events directly related to the case.

To call such underlying premises used in making inferences about a mystery a *theoretical* framework may sound strange, because usually we talk about theory when referring to a systematic set of explicitly stated hypotheses or assumptions. However, here it is not expected that investigators are conscious of the premises underlying their inferences. As was pointed out, observations are always theory-laden. In scientific research investigators are supposed to become conscious of and reflect on their premises, but that is also common in detective stories: a new insight into a mystery is often gained by the detective questioning a self-evident underlying assumption.

The theoretical framework always influences the choice of methods. Detective stories, for instance, have, since the heyday of Conan Doyle and Agatha Christie, moved increasingly towards psychological problematics: the mystery in present-day detective stories is not so much the murderer's identity as the murderer's motives and personality. The chief method employed by Georges Simenon's Superintendent Maigret, for instance, is to gather impressions about the milieu around the scene of the crime, about its people and their ways of thinking. Maigret situates the crime and the personality of the criminal against the social and cultural background out of which they have grown.

In the context of social research the theoretical framework is not merely a list of possible explanations to be tested in the search for a solution, but a way of perceiving the reality under study. The researcher who is making observations and inferences may well find new models of explanation that are compatible with the theoretical framework employed. In fact the solution to any single case is always to some extent unique.

Take Agatha Christie's short story *A Pocket Full of Rye*. In this story Miss Marple organizes the clues she has picked up according to the nursery rhyme 'Sing a Song of Sixpence', which includes a pocket full of rye, blackbirds baked in a pie, a king, honey and a maid in the garden. It turns out that the murders in this case have followed these 'predictions'. However, rather than serving as a model of explanation, the nursery rhyme merely paves the way to the next question: what is the murderer trying to achieve with this 'playfulness'?

From specific to generic, from generic to specific

In concrete, individual cases it is difficult to identify the theoretical framework that the researcher has chosen, the method that is applied or the different models that are tested in the search for an explanation. An explicit description of the theoretical framework applied will only be given in social scientific studies. In detective stories the way of perceiving the world is more or less commonsensical. However, detective stories are useful for purposes of tracing the process of deduction from observations to the final solution of the case.

Sherlock Holmes, who is always explaining his method to Dr Watson, describes it as a form of deductive reasoning, although philosophers (Eco and Sebeok 1983) who have studied Holmes' cases say it actually represents the model of abductive reasoning. For the present purposes it makes little difference which theoretical concept is used to describe the method of the detective story. However, an examination of the different stages involved should be useful.

In detective stories the process of drawing conclusions involves two elements. It proceeds both from the specific to the generic and vice versa. Observable details are examined in order to see how they might be connected to some wider context. On the other hand, new observations are collected and weighed against the initial hypothesis thus constructed, to see whether they could corroborate the solution proposed.

There is no set order in which these two stages appear, but they come alternately, one after the other. The choice of a given model of explanation, the testing of this model and the formation of a new model amount to a hermeneutic cycle which leads eventually to the final solution. On the one hand, it is impossible to know in advance how the problem will be resolved without the researcher collecting observations and trying to sort out what they suggest. On the other hand, the observations are only relevant when they are examined as clues, i.e. when they are taken as evidence of a chain of events or a phenomenon that could explain the problem in hand. However, it is only rarely that the solution is found the first time round; typically the process will involve various steps of trial and error. If, for instance, a given model of explanation, a given hypothesis, provides a logical explanation to most clues, then the researcher can go back to reconsider the observations for which no explanation was forthcoming, to try to find out whether the meaning of those observations could be interpreted in some other way so that they would fit into the emerging picture. If this does not work, then an entirely new explanatory model will be needed so that the observations can be reinterpreted from that perspective.

It is the researcher's job to decide how the clues are to be interpreted so that they amount to a logical construct. If a logical explanation is found, then it will lend further credence to the clues. When the solution which is proposed is considered correct, the clues speaking in favour of that solution will often be described with a different word: they are now regarded as *evidence*.

Clues and evidence

In crime stories all evidence is considered with suspicion and humility. It is precisely the ambivalence of facts that makes them so interesting, as Raymond Chandler's character Philip Marlowe notes in *Farewell, My Lovely*:

> 'Proof,' I said, 'is always a relative thing. It's an overwhelming balance of probabilities. And that's a matter of how they strike you.'

However, the drawing of conclusions is more than just guess-work; some conclusions are always more reliable than others. Crudely speaking, the greater the number of clues which support the solution of the mystery, i.e. which serve as evidence in favour of the solution, the more likely it is that the solution is the right one.

Let us turn to Conan Doyle again for an example. In 'The Adventure of the Yellow Face', Sherlock Holmes is visited by a man who is concerned about his wife. She had lived previously in America and got married there. She had moved back to England and taken up residence in Norbury, where her first husband and children had died of yellow fever. After three years of a perfectly happy marriage, the man's wife had started to behave quite strangely. Two months previously she had asked her husband for a hundred pounds, without any explanation. Now, she has secretly gone into a previously unoccupied house nearby. In the window the man had seen a strange, yellow livid face. On the basis of what he hears Holmes deduces that the wife's first husband has not in fact died. Instead, the wife has for some reason run away and changed her name. Now, the first husband has found out her whereabouts and has started to blackmail her. However, he is not content with the amount of money he has received and has turned up in a nearby house to threaten her with a scandal.

Holmes asks Dr Watson what he thinks of his theory; it is all surmise, the doctor says. 'But at least it covers all the facts,' Holmes replies. 'When new facts come to our knowledge which cannot be covered by it, it will be time enough to reconsider it.'

Holmes' solution is not based on any given theory of typical crimes or characteristics of criminals, for instance, although such theories are no doubt an important asset in the interpretation of the observations presented to him, in the translation of these observations into clues. The most important thing is to create a logical model of explanation within which all pieces of the jigsaw will snap into place.

However, in this particular story it turns out that the jigsaw is not big enough. The strange face in the window is in fact the woman's child who is wearing a mask. The child has not died after all, but the woman has kept her existence a secret from her new husband. This time another logical model emerges, providing an adequate explanation for the pieces of the jigsaw. Given the surprising outcome Holmes, in a rare display of humility, acknowledges the wide array of possible solutions that this sort of case may present:

> 'Watson,' said he, 'if it should ever strike you that I am getting a little overconfident in my powers, or giving less pains to a case than it deserves, kindly whisper "Norbury" in my ear, and I shall be infinitely obliged to you.'

Detective stories, common sense and social research

The difference between clues and evidence helps to clarify the difference between detective stories and social research. The model of inference applied in detective stories differs from many of the examples that are found in the social sciences in that crime writers expose the train of thought in much greater detail, including all the various stages of trial and error. The reader becomes involved in the unfolding mystery from the very outset. In the detective story observations are examined as clues pointing to different possible explanations. In the social sciences, by contrast, hardly ever is the whole process of inference documented; instead the observations are straightaway presented from the point of view of the model of explanation that has proved most viable: the observations are examined as evidence. There are, of course, differences in this regard between different lines of inquiry in the social sciences. For instance, statistical social research will not normally look at the empirical material collected from any other angle than how far it supports the hypothesis set out at the beginning of the report. Qualitative research, on the other hand, will typically begin with more descriptive accounts and less interpretation. However, the description of the material needs to follow certain principles of economy: it is not generally considered acceptable to describe at the beginning such things that have nothing whatsoever to do with the solution that is presented at the end of the study. One feature that these two types of empirical social research do have in common, in spite of their differences in mode of presentation, is that trials and errors are hardly ever documented. Reference may be made to alternative interpretations, but this will merely serve the purpose of demonstrating that these alternatives are not applicable in the light of the evidence in hand.

But the mode of presentation remains a secondary issue. The most important thing is that the process of deduction in social research is very similar to the corresponding process in detective stories. The research process, whether it concerns society or crimes, proceeds alternately in two different directions, from the specific to the generic and from the generic to the specific, until eventually a final solution is reached. The differences between the end-products of crime stories and social research are due mainly to the fact that in the latter category only success stories get published, i.e. those which corroborate the model of explanation with which the researcher started out. This is achieved by restricting the presentation of the material to those questions for which the material provides a justified explanation.

Another difference between detective stories and social research is that the latter relies to a great extent on the accumulation of knowledge. Individual research reports often refer to earlier studies in the choice of a model of explanation or line of argumentation. Solutions to various research problems often produce new information that other scholars can apply in tackling new problems. Earlier results may also be quoted as evidence of the validity of the solution proposed. It is for this reason that some reports in social research seem to amount to little more than an empirical test of a preset hypothesis, even though the process has in fact involved various steps of trial and error and an analysis of earlier studies on the topic concerned.

The tendency for social scientific knowledge to accumulate is explained by the way that social research formulates its research problems. Although empirical research is often concerned with a specific phenomenon or individual case, it is primarily interested in whether the solution also applies to other corresponding phenomena. The social sciences are expected to produce universally valid findings, empirical or theoretical generalizability. An individual occurrence or the fates of individuals will only be of interest to the social sciences if it is demonstrated that the occurrence or individual in question represents a 'typical case', or if it is shown that the occurrence will have an impact on the lives of large numbers of people. In these cases the general interest is based on empirical generalizability. On the other hand, an individual or deviant phenomenon may have scientific relevance if the analysis of that phenomenon paves the way to a new perception of society. In the latter case the general interest-value of the study will depend on how well it corroborates the model of explanation and theoretical framework applied in the study.

The knowledge that is produced by research arriving at theoretical generalizations is not of a cumulative nature; it does not complement or support existing knowledge structures, but on the contrary undermines them. A new explanation of a given phenomenon that is based on an analysis of an individual case will make it necessary to construct a new critical approach towards the 'facts' and 'evidence' that have been constructed on the basis of earlier theoretical frameworks and explanatory models. A theoretical discovery will cause a break that leads towards a new stage of knowledge accumulation, i.e. to the empirical testing of a theoretical framework.

Regardless of whether social research provides supportive or complementary evidence to existing knowledge or whether it undermines and criticizes that knowledge, it is always characterized by a close relationship to existing, well-known theories and ways of thought. Although social research is concerned to resolve an endless chain of individual mysteries (just as detective stories), the underlying set of issues, of big questions that are shared in common by different studies, is in the end comparatively limited. The social sciences search for and comment upon social life in different ways.

The social sciences seek to test and shatter accustomed ways of thinking, and to wage rational debate about questions that concern society. This debate is not necessarily more clever or more creative than that waged among 'ordinary' people. The social sciences have no monopoly on reflective thinking concerning social issues. Besides, it is not individuals' wit but rather the objective of doing social research which is at stake here. Social research has to justify its arguments, refer to its observations in support of what it has said. In so far as the purpose of research is not only to provide a description of events or to chart their prevalence but also to find better ways of understanding and explaining them, it cannot confine itself to everyday explanations and frameworks. It must constantly question these explanations and frames and make visible the premises on which they are based. Otherwise social research would not be able to say anything we did not know already.[1]

Although the social sciences do not distance themselves from everyday assumptions and commonsensical frameworks, they cannot confine themselves to everyday-life discourses. The different schools of social sciences can be described as systems of assumptions and explanations about reality. To an extent these theoretical frameworks can call into question the matters of course of everyday experience. More important than that, however, is for the different lines of social scientific inquiry to take critical distance from individual observations, examining them at another level of generality.

In practice this often means that research produces its own observations that are dependent on the observations of individual people, but nonetheless take distance from them. For instance, survey questionnaires start out from information provided by the respondents and their reported views on things, but for the researcher the basic observations consist of the

---

1.　However, the impression one gets when reading the results of different studies is that this is precisely what has happened in most cases. This does not mean to say that the social sciences should not set more ambitious goals for themselves. The purpose of opinion polls and various government or market surveys is obviously not to find new ways of thinking, but simply to measure the frequency of different phenomena and the number of people behaving in different ways.

distributions of preset responses and the statistical associations between different responses. The researcher's clues consist of the observations based on these analyses, not of the observations made by the interviewees.

The methods of producing observations are an integral part of the theoretical models applied in research, which by and large determine what kind of phenomena and what sort of observations about those phenomena are relevant to the explanation of social reality. However, not nearly all schools of social thought have their own methodology that is derived from a theoretical framework. In fact the historical evidence shows that there are only a handful of methods of data collection that have evolved with the development of modern society and that have opened up new ways of perceiving society and of explaining its phenomena. For instance, empirical social research began with the translation of social reality into figures, measures and weights. This decision in itself involved many assumptions about the general nature and meaning of the observations collected, at the same time as it created various theoretical models within which the material collected was interpreted.

CHAPTER 4

THE QUANTIFYING METHOD

The classical period of sociology in the late nineteenth and early twentieth centuries was a point of confluence for many different lines of social research and social philosophy. Works by the great seminal figures of sociology combined elements from classical political economy, German philosophy, empirical social research and official statistics. At the same time sociology became institutionalized, increasingly distancing itself from the disciplines that were its roots: it was now to stand apart as a fully fledged academic discipline, distinct from 'empiricist' and bureaucratic fiddling with government statistics. It is for this reason that so little is known about the contributions of many classic authors such as Max Weber and Ferdinand Tönnies to the development of the methods of quantitative social research (Oberschall 1965). The seminal authors are chiefly remembered for their 'theoretical' work, i.e. for the results of their research rather than for the methods which led them to their discoveries.

It is hard to find a name to describe a basic strategy of social research that is not already loaded with meanings. To avoid the immediate connotations and interpretations that would be evoked by a label from the existing nomenclature, I have chosen to call the methodology that is described in this chapter 'the quantifying method'. The purest applications are perhaps to be found in the research tradition known as 'statistical social research' or 'survey analysis' (Rosenberg 1968), but the basic methodological principles are the same throughout most of the field of social research.

The label I propose does not mean to say that the research material for this line of inquiry consists exclusively or even primarily of figures and statistics. Rather, the term refers to the operations in and through which the observations concerning reality are produced. The quantifying method looks at reality as a system of laws composed of different kinds of 'variables'. Its main tools of analysis are standardization and the explanation of differences.

The influential studies by Karl Marx and Émile Durkheim that are discussed in this chapter are good examples of the use of the quantifying method. Creative and ingenious applications of the method, these works demonstrate how it can be used to produce truly useful results.

The quantifying method is one of the tools available to the researcher for purposes of abstracting from reality, from manifest observations in their given form. A measure of intellectual audacity and imagination is always required for resolving emerging problems and mysteries: the researcher must step back and take distance from conventional views of the connections between things. The process of abstraction also involves making various generalizations and basic assumptions. When William Petty, a founding member of political arithmetic, said he would leave causes 'that depend upon mutable Minds, Opinions, Appetites, and Passions of particular Men, to the consideration of others', he at once had to make the assumption that these factors were not relevant at the level of abstraction he had chosen. The choice of a 'level of abstraction' requires a knowledge of other possible 'levels', an overall understanding of the slice of reality that is under investigation. These basic assumptions that are characteristic of the quantifying method have two consequences. Firstly, the results may only be weighed in the context of the world-view that lies behind the theoretical framework applied in the study: if that world-view is not accepted, then the results must also be re-examined from a different vantage-point. Secondly, the level of abstraction imposes its own limits on the applicability of the research results: for instance, no conclusions can be drawn from Petty's studies about people's mentalities.

In order to assess the applicability of a given research method, one needs to have at least a basic knowledge of the presumptions and premises entailed by that method or approach about the reality that is being studied. There is a brief discussion at the end of this chapter about the basic premises of the quantifying method.

Political economy and Marx

Karl Marx's (1818–1883) *Capital: A Critique of Political Economy* is an outstanding piece of research, particularly in terms of the analytical accuracy with which the 'experimental design' for the study is set up. Various steps of complex abstractions precede the analysis in which Marx uncovers the 'essence' of the phenomenon he is studying.

Marx's focal concern is with the economy of capitalist society. In this regard he is following up the work of the tradition of political economy that started in the eighteenth century. On the other hand, Marx's analysis also integrates influences from German idealism and particularly Hegel; in this regard he considerably expands the traditional concept of the economy and its significance to social development. It follows that Marx is also considered a seminal figure in sociology.

Following the tradition of classical political economy, Marx is not interested in a detailed analysis of the motives of individual activity. This is not out of ignorance, however; the reason lies in Marx's choice to focus on the systemic entity of actions in which human individuals engage. Marx was well aware of the implications of his presumptions and the limitations that the setting imposed on his work. Unlike the analysis of natural phenomena, the analysis of economic forms benefits neither from microscopes nor from chemical reagents: 'The power of abstraction must replace both' (Marx 1977 [1867], 90). In the Preface to the first edition of *Capital*, Marx also makes it clear what sort of abstraction he has made in order to uncover the laws of movement of capitalist society:

> I do not by any means depict the capitalist and the landowner in rosy colours. But individuals are dealt with here only in so far as they are the personifications of economic categories, the bearers of particular class relations and interests. (ibid., 92)

Marx reduces individuals, their interests and pursuits, to representatives of certain class interests. There is also another way in which individuals are present only as abstractions. This is clear from the very outset of Marx's work, where he introduces the reader to the theme of his study, i.e. the economy:

> The wealth of societies in which the capitalist mode of production prevails appears as an 'immense collection of commodities'; the individual commodity appears as its elementary form. Our investigation therefore begins with the analysis of the commodity.
> The commodity is, first of all, an external object, a thing which through its qualities satisfies human needs of whatever kind. The nature of these needs, whether they arise, for example, from the stomach, or the imagination, makes no difference. Nor does it matter here how the thing satisfies man's need, whether directly as a means of subsistence, i.e. an object of consumption, or indirectly as a means of production. (ibid., 125)

Marx leaves aside more detailed reflections about the motives for different actions; to him they are irrelevant. Instead, he is interested in capitalist society as a whole, something that is 'no solid crystal, but an organism capable of change, and constantly engaged in a process of change' (ibid., 93). The only relevant motives, therefore, are the 'needs' of individuals, whatever their origin. Further, since 'commodities', in capitalism, satisfy the needs of individuals, the law of movement of the capitalist mode of production can be studied by applying the methods of mathematics and statistics to an analysis of economic parameters, prices and wages as well as statistics describing the living conditions of the working class: 'the exploitation of women and children, the conditions of housing and nourishment and so on' (ibid., 91).

However, Marx does not content himself with this abstraction from the level of motives for individual actions. To reach his ultimate goal, the embryonic form of the capitalist mode of production, he executes a major, highly complex abstraction. Marx is not interested in prices and wages *per se*, for these will not suffice to uncover the innermost essence of capitalist society. Through his abstractions Marx coins a set of basic concepts that he can use to describe the economy. He explores the wealth of capitalist society from the vantage-point of its manifestation, i.e. the commodity. But for Marx, the commodity is more than just a manifestation of wealth; using the power of abstraction as a microscope, he argues that the commodity can be examined as the embryonic form of the whole capitalist mode of production. This, in turn, paves the way to an examination of how value, as reflected in the price of the commodity, is determined in each case.

In order to locate the ultimate source and origin of value, Marx applies a statistical procedure to abstract from everyday reality: he *standardizes* the effect of factors that could interfere with observations of the phenomenon studied, such as variations in demand and supply and differences between different lines of production. It is this stripped-down model of capitalism that Marx explores throughout *Capital*, all the way to the last chapters of Volume 3. Given this model, he can concentrate his analysis on one single *capital* which owns the means of production and which generates surplus-value; on one impersonal *labour force* which earns a certain *wage*; and on one single *commodity*, which is sold for its *value* and which satisfies all of people's needs.

Within this setting Marx contrives to demonstrate that the wage paid to the labourer is not in fact the value of the labour expended, but the *value of the hired labour power*. In this sense the value of labour power is not determined by the value of the labour input during the working day or the value that is materialized in the commodities produced, but by the costs of labour reproduction. In other words, the wage labourer's pay is determined according to the amount of money that the average labourer needs in order to provide a living not only for himself, but also for his offspring – and in this way to guarantee the availability of labour power in the future. In Marx's day, the average wage level was based on the cultural assumption that a male family breadwinner is able to support his family.

The most important thing about this solution of Marx's is that it constitutes an internally logical system: starting out from an examination of statistics and economic parameters, he reconstructs a systemic model which observes, and which will continue to observe, its own inherent laws so long as there exist in the world representatives of the role characters identified, or what Marx calls 'economic character masks': owners of the means of production, i.e. capital, and labour power or wage labourers. Marx does not need to assume that his systemic model will only work on condition that some of the role characters will cheat; on the contrary, each stage in the circulation process of capital is based on an exchange of equal values. The fact that the capitalist class, the representative of capital, 'expropriates' the surplus-value generated is based on the simple fact that the amount of wage paid to labourers is not determined by the value of the labour expended, but by the value required for labour reproduction. All of this is of course grounded in the historical premise that there exists one group of people who own the means of production, and another group of people who own nothing else than their labour power.

Durkheim and statistical analysis

Another seminal figure in sociology who has made an interesting and significant contribution to the development of the quantifying method is Émile Durkheim. In *Suicide* (1966 [1897]), Durkheim marries academic sociology with empirical, quantitative social research (e.g. French and German moral statistics). In terms of its method, *Suicide* closely resembles the approaches that are applied in modern statistical social research, and the way in which the observations are organized into an internally logical and theoretically coherent system is still a textbook example.

At first glance the subject of the study, i.e. suicide, does not seem a particularly relevant choice for a sociologist who is interested in the laws of community and social life: surely this is very much an individual matter, an act of an individual with few if any effects beyond that individual. Durkheim does not deny that each suicide has its own personal history which may help to explain the individual's decision and actions. However, he goes on to demonstrate that the occurrence of suicides is ultimately determined by social facts produced by the structure of social life. The number of suicides in each society is more or less constant and changes only very slowly from year to year: it is a social fact which for its own part reflects the distinctiveness of each society in relation to other societies.

From these vantage-points Durkheim proceeds to a statistical analysis of suicide, looking at how the total number of suicides varies over time and between different countries and different regions; and at how it varies in different religions, between men and women, in different age groups and marital status groups, and by level of education. He concludes that the system of social facts he has unearthed is not explained by psychopathic conditions, by race or heritage, by cosmic factors or imitation. Rather, the clues suggest that the explanation for the links between the suicide rate at any given time with the background variables mentioned is to be found in the nature of suicide as a social phenomenon.

Durkheim discovered that the suicide rates at different times and in different institutions and their variation is explained by different factors. From this it can be inferred that there exist different types of suicide, of which Durkheim distinguished three principal ones: the *egoistic* suicide, in which the person no longer has any reason to live; the *altruistic* suicide, in which the community obliges its member to commit suicide; and *anomic* suicide, which is explained by the lack of regulation of human activity. According to Durkheim, altruistic suicides occur primarily in primitive societies where the individual is very much an integral part of the community and therefore does not carry very much value. Egoistic and anomic suicide, by contrast, are characteristic of modern society.

Through the concept of anomie, Durkheim extends the scope of his study way beyond its apparent topic: the theme that emerges at the centre of attention is the Industrial Revolution in Western societies and the changes caused by this process in the collective consciousness. Like other classical sociologists, Durkheim is concerned to explore the social changes that created the sociological imagination and the object of sociology, i.e. modern society. Durkheim's interpretation is that many social problems (such as suicides) are due to an erosion of shared values, which in turn is explained by an erosion of traditional social bonds. People are left alone to face the task of defining their own values and to find a meaning for life. In this situation they may no longer want to live on or to respect the life and values of others.

The experimental design

The method that Durkheim used in his study is a good example of the procedures of statistical social research, of the way in which it forces answers out of reality. The aim is to get as close as possible to the classical experimental design that is familiar from the natural sciences. In the classical, controlled experiment the researcher starts out with a hypothesis according to which the *independent* variable influences the *dependent* variable. If the study is concerned with, say, the impacts of cognitive behaviour therapy upon the treatment of alcoholism, the independent variable would be a certain form of therapy and the dependent variable the outcome of therapy, measured, for instance, on the basis of physiological tests which reveal excessive alcohol consumption. The experiment itself is so conducted that the researcher first picks out two groups that resemble each other as closely as possible, an *experimental group* and a *control group*, and then measures the value of the dependent variable in each group. In the example just described this could mean that the physiological tests mentioned are conducted on the people in both groups admitted to therapy for alcohol problems. The independent variable is then inserted into the experimental group but not in the control group: in other words, the members of the experimental group continue to receive regular institutional treatment but additionally go to behavioural therapy, whereas the controls only receive regular treatment. Finally, the value of the dependent variable is measured in both groups. In this case the subjects in both groups would take part in a follow-up measurement in, say, six months' time. This paves the way to testing the hypothesis: when the value of the change in the dependent variable in the control group is deducted from the corresponding change in the experimental group, the result will indicate the effect of the independent variable. In this example the indicator of treatment results would be the changes in the results of physiological measurements during the six-month period, and the impact of the therapy would be defined as the difference between the results for the experimental group and the control group.

The main idea of the scientific experiment, and at once its main problem, is that all external factors are bracketed out:

every effort must be made to control for those factors. This means, for instance, that the two groups just mentioned, the experimental group and control group, should resemble each other as closely as possible. This in itself is extremely difficult in a study involving human individuals. Another problem involved in the study of humans is that the motivation of the people who have been selected to try out a new therapy may in fact be the most important explanatory factor of all. In medicine and experimental psychology this factor is known as the placebo effect. One way in which researchers have tried to control this effect is to form a third group in which the members are recruited into another new therapy which sounds equally credible (Koski-Jännes 1992).

There are also ethical problems to be considered. In therapy research the control group will normally continue to receive 'regular treatment' rather than having treatment withheld altogether. However, it is obvious that there are numerous social phenomena that cannot be studied within an experimental setting. Consider, for instance, arranging an experiment to see how children are affected by losing their father: the researcher cannot phone up the fathers of the children recruited into the experimental group and tell them to disappear for a few years (Eskola 1971, 156–157). Nor is it possible to investigate the reasons for suicide in two groups, an experimental group and a control group. This is why the experimental design is constructed in conceptual terms, by way of abstraction, by studying two groups drawn from different statistics or registers and resembling each other as closely as possible, except that the members of one group have committed suicide. In this sense it may be argued that statistical social research is based on *ex post facto* experiments, i.e. that they use designs set up after the events.

This is what Durkheim did in his study discussed above – even though he did not make direct comparisons between people who had committed suicide and people who had died of some other cause at the individual level, but examined different dependent variables that explained the suicide rates. Some of these analyses had to do with differences in the incidence of suicides between different population groups; others had to do with changes influencing the number of suicides, which affect the same population at different points in time. The basic idea

Table 4.1   The effect of the Paris World Exposition 1889 on
suicide rates in Paris

	1888	1889	1890
The seven months of the Exposition	517	567	540
The five other months	319	311	356

Source: Durkheim 1966, 245

in all these cases is the same: having controlled for other factors, the researcher can look at the impacts of the independent variable upon the dependent variable.

In fact every tabular analysis in quantitative social research can be seen as an imitation of the classical scientific experiment. Let us look at one of Durkheim's tables in which he demonstrates the impact of the 1889 Paris World Exposition on the number of suicides (see Table 4.1).

Durkheim used these figures to show that during the seven months of the World Exposition in 1889, the number of suicides increased by almost 10 per cent; no such increase occurred during the corresponding months either in the previous year or in the year after the World Exposition. The figures for the number of suicides during the five other months in the three years concerned indicate that the increase occurred precisely during the Exposition. In other words the table in question is based on an experimental design in which the experimental group is represented by the Parisian population during the seven months of the 1889 World Exposition, while the control group consists of the same population during other periods in 1888–1890. The independent variable is the World Exposition and the dependent variable the number of suicides.

From interview responses to observations

Although an extremely competent piece of work and in many respects quite ingenious, Durkheim's study was still rather crude in comparison with the sophisticated methods of present-day statistical social research. Durkheim did not (any more than any other sociologist around the turn of the century) calculate correlations between different variables, even though the method was by this time known in statistics (Kent 1981; Selvin 1985). It was not until the 1930s and after the Second World War when sampling methods, attitude measurements based on survey interviews and more advanced methods of statistics were introduced that things began to change more dramatically (Lazarsfeld 1968).

Modern statistical methods have opened up various new ways in which to search for and describe the statistical associations between variables, yet the methodological foundations of statistical research have remained essentially unchanged. One of the new methodological innovations is the use of interviews and self-administered questionnaires for purposes of data collection. Firstly, this involves the theory of a sample which represents the population. Secondly, the idea that interview responses are treated as observations that describe the characteristics of the individuals randomly selected to the sample requires several steps of abstraction and standardization. Likewise, the method of attitude measurements, i.e. that attitudes and behaviours are explained by the respondents' age, sex, occupational status or other constant characteristics of individuals, requires many further implicit or explicit assumptions about the nature of the reality investigated.

Let us begin by looking at the assumptions that lie behind the sampling method. This method is grounded in the requirement of statistical generalizability: since the purpose of social scientific research is in most cases to draw generalizable conclusions, survey interviews will aim to do this by demarcating the group of people, the *population*, to which the results should apply. The population is rarely defined as comprising humankind in its entirety, but it could consist of the British population or women living in London, for instance. Since it is rarely possible to study all people in the population, a *sample* will have to be drawn. Various statistical methods such as random sampling are used to make sure that the sample is maximally representative of the population.

More specifically, the sample represents the population with respect to certain criteria or variables. The population is a theoretical concept in so far as it is defined on the basis of certain concepts or variables, based on geographical region or gender or age group. In this sense the existing practical and theoretical knowledge that the researcher brings to the social survey will influence the making of observations even at the stage where the population is demarcated, long before the issue of sample representativity is addressed or before the presumptions involved in the drawing of statistical conclusions are analysed.

Abstraction from everyday observations is also required at the stage where questions and preset responses are formulated for survey analysis. To design a good questionnaire the researcher needs to have a fairly good and comprehensive knowledge of the research problem and to anticipate what sort of hypotheses will be tested with the material. There are of course various background items that are asked more or less routinely in questionnaires (such as the respondent's age, sex, marital status and occupation), primarily for purposes of describing the group recruited. These data are also useful for comparisons with the whole population and hence for assessments of sample representativity. However, the most important consideration of all is *research economy*. Background information on individuals and questions about people's attitudes are not asked just for the fun of it: the inclusion of each and every item in the questionnaire must be motivated by an expectation that the material obtained will be relevant to the topic of the study. For every question written down, the researcher must have some preconception as to what sort of variables the responses will be compared against.

The nature of these anticipated analyses will also largely determine what sort of typology of preset responses is used in the questionnaire. For example, there is no point in asking the respondents to describe their daily viewing habits by type of programme genre down to each quarter of an hour if television viewing is a secondary concern in relation to the study topic proper. The size of the sample may also restrict the range of preset responses: if it is to be expected that the number of observations in many categories will remain below statistical significance, then obviously it is a waste of time to create an overly pedantic classification.

The definition of the preset responses for questionnaires is in itself a process of measurement. It is a basic requirement that the response options are sensitive. If the population is defined as consisting of the female population of London, for instance, then there is no point in including a question on the respondents' sex or place of residence; and it is equally futile to look at the breakdown of other responses and their statistical associations with these variables. Equally useless is the question to which all respondents give the same answer: although it may be interesting to find a feature or an opinion that is shared in common by all women in London, this sort of finding could not be *explained* by means of statistical research.

The questionnaire form is a kind of screen or magnifying glass which describes the subjects in a predetermined manner. When the material is collected, i.e. when the questionnaire items are completed with data describing the individual respondents, new presumptions will have to be made again. The *self-administered questionnaire* and the *interview* are different from each other in this respect. Both in the interview situation where the respondent answers the questions orally and in the case of a self-administered questionnaire where the respondent answers the questions in writing, the methodological principle of statistical social research requires that all factors which may influence the responses must be controlled for and standardized as far as possible. The response situation should be as identical as possible for all respondents: for instance, the presence of other family members in the same room is not normally allowed during the interview (unless this is specifically required). The best results as far as standardization is concerned are achieved in a situation where all the subjects are in the same room for the duration of the interview. In psychological experiments, interviews and other observations concerning the subject's behaviour are sometimes carried out in a laboratory setting. It is also important that all subjects receive the same introduction to the study and that the instructions are given in the same way. Often the interviewer will read exactly the same instructions, word for word, to all subjects.

It is obviously not possible to have identical interview situations for all interviewees. If, for instance, the data are collected by several interviewers, the responses may be influenced by their personality or gender. These kinds of uncontrolled factors should be coded so that their impact on the responses can be controlled afterwards when the results are analysed. If it is indicated, for instance, whether the interviews were conducted by a man or a woman, it is possible to measure the impact of this factor on the responses.

So there are two principles here: the aim, on the one hand, is to minimize interference and, on the other hand, to control for intervening factors. Ideally, the research setting should not change the reality that is under investigation. The principle is the same as in the measurement of an electric voltage: the instrument gives a slightly reduced reading owing to the minimal current that passes through the instrument, but this can be taken into account when the instrument is calibrated.

It is no coincidence that the method of producing observations in survey analysis resembles the methods of measurement applied in physics: statistical social research is modelled on the natural scientific experiment in this regard, too. However, the phenomena measured in social research are very different in comparison with physical phenomena. When in social research the questions are worded in exactly the same way and presented to the respondents in as similar situations as possible in order to try to eliminate the effects of measurement, the inherent assumption is that a question which is worded in exactly the same way is a similar 'stimulus' to all respondents. Observations are accordingly examined as 'reactions' of different individuals to the same stimulus.

This methodological premise of survey analysis is of course paradoxical in view of the concerns of these studies, which most typically are with the way in which people weigh and interpret and evaluate different things, the way in which they act and behave in the reality that they themselves, in part, produce through their activity. To the researcher who is designing a survey, all of this is merely a nuisance factor and a potential source of errors, a problem that needs to be resolved. Again there are bound to be ethical problems: sometimes interviewees are misled or told only part of the truth, because if they knew the true purpose of the study, that might interfere with their responses. The real paradox, however, is that the survey is concerned to produce observations of individuals who have been stripped as far as possible of everything that is considered relevant to the object of study, i.e. social reality and the human individual as a cultural creature.

The limits and possibilities of the survey

There is nothing extraordinary about this paradox. If the researcher is to make accurate, perceptive observations and inferences from everyday observations, they must be abstracted from; the observations must be examined from a perspective that makes it possible to explain the problems studied. This is precisely how reality is forced to answer the questions presented by the researcher. The point that needs to be stressed is that the survey produces observations that are constructed in a specific manner. Knowledge of the presumptions that are typical of this construction will help both to draw conclusions about the applicability of the method to a particular study and to recognize the limits of this method.

So what exactly are the limits of survey methodology? Textbooks on quantitative social research often say that the purpose of research which works with survey interview materials is to extract *universally valid laws*, to identify the *causes* of things. The direction of the causal relationship is usually ascertained by designating certain permanent characteristics of individuals (sex, place of residence, age or marital status) as an independent variable and certain actions (such as voting decisions) or personality characteristics (such as authoritarianism or alienation) as a dependent variable.

Accordingly, the purpose of the next step – a closer statistical analysis of the material – is to make sure that the causal relationships discovered are genuine and not due to a third variable. Rosenberg (1968, 24–26) has an example in which listening to religious radio programmes is studied by trying to identify the characteristics of individuals which explain the amount of listening. When it turns out that old people listen to religious programmes more often than young people, the next step is to control for the effect of other possible variables. It now transpires that the explanatory variable is in fact education. The correlation detected between age and listenership for religious radio programmes was due to the fact that older age groups are on average less educated than young people. So eventually, the analysis yielded a reliable, genuine causal relationship.

The discovery of a solid causal relationship is an important finding in so far as the purpose of the research is to collect hard 'facts' in support of practical decision-making. For instance, an organization that wants to do an advertising campaign on the radio might infer from the evidence above that the best way to reach people with a low level of education is to insert the commercials in-between religious programmes. Yet in more general terms the interest-value of such a finding is limited. It says nothing at all about the connection between educational level and religious programmes, even though it may inspire the imagination. It would be easy to extend the chain of causal relationships. What is it in education that makes people less interested in religion or religious radio programmes? Or conversely: why do people who drop out of school or who are unable to continue their studies take an interest in religion? Or does the causal relationship possibly work the other way round: perhaps it is the religious conviction that explains the decision to drop out of school?

The longer the chains of causal relationships, the more often one will find situations where different variables appear as both causes and consequences, depending on which is chosen as the dependent and which as the independent variable. Alex Inkeles (1969), for instance, concluded that education is the most important factor in explaining what makes the people of developing countries 'modern'; whereas Claud Sutcliffe (1978) concluded that *father's* education and future orientation is the most significant independent variable in explaining whose children are sent to school in the first place.

Although the search for causal relationships is an important part of statistical social research, the tracing of causal chains is by no means something that the method itself necessitates.[1] Many sociologists believe that the discovery of logically distinct 'independent' and 'dependent' variables is merely the vantage-point for interpretation; that logical causal relationships are merely clues that need to be scrutinized in closer detail to

---

1. Although it is very common. Statistical social research is quite firm in its belief that the ultimate explanation for things, more often than not, can be extracted mathematically. For instance, it is assumed that the ultimate source, the original cause for everything, lies somewhere along the causal chain: it is merely a matter of going back far enough. Another version of this same thought-model is to try to find systemic models that describe the totality of causal chains which are either mutually reinforcing or which act in different directions. This could be described as a cybernetic attempt at a solution.

extract a sociological explanation. This is the position that Durkheim represents with his suicide study: he is not content simply to present his 'discoveries' of causal relationships; instead, these have a secondary role as evidence in the systemic model of society that he is defending in the study.[2]

A useful example at this juncture is Pierre Bourdieu's *Distinction* (1984), a study which is based on survey data. Bourdieu, however, is interested less in examining the statistical '*significantness*' than the sociological '*significance*' of statistical relationships: what are the 'sociologically intelligible constant relationships which are simultaneously revealed and concealed in the statistical relationships between a given indicator and different practices' (ibid., 22)? He throws overboard the whole notion of universal causal relationships. Unlike the statistician and formal logician, Bourdieu does not take the individual's characteristics (occupation, age, gender, educational level) as given, as 'explanatory factors', as if they were balls on a snooker table knocking each other around. Rather, he looks at the statistical associations between 'characteristics' and different practices and tastes as indications of the existence of different 'habituses', i.e. certain ways of thinking and patterns of behaviour. His theory is that within each 'field' in society, people collect and accumulate the type of capital that is most valuable in this particular field. This is not, however, a conscious pursuit of personal gain; rather, the collection of different types of capital is, in a cultural sense, an unconscious activity. As far as the individual is concerned, it is simply a matter of leading a good and meaningful life according to the ways of thinking and tastes acquired in the childhood home.

---

2. This ideal is so widely espoused in sociological research that it has come to influence the entire vocabulary of social research. 'Empirical' refers to statistical discoveries, 'theoretical' to the frameworks within which sociological explanations are offered for the 'empirical'. 'Theoretical research' is accordingly often taken to mean the testing of different kinds of explanations in the light of research carried out by others and secondary analyses, whereas 'empirical research' refers to research which looks at 'empirical material' specifically collected for that study. These distinctions may be useful for crude practical purposes of classifying different types of research, but the fact remains that 'empirical facts' are always theoretical, and 'theories' always empirical.

One of the most important institutions where people can collect cultural capital, Bourdieu says, is the school. Educational capital can then be used to 'purchase' other forms of capital, for instance economic capital. Although schools do not actually teach good taste in art, this is nonetheless an important part of the influence of education over and above the official curriculum. In French society there prevails an ideology of equality according to which the opportunity to have an education or to acquire other forms of capital should not depend on personal wealth but entirely on 'talent'.

However, referring to his statistical data, Bourdieu demonstrates that the ability to make use of education, to exchange educational capital at the best possible rate for cultural capital, is dependent on social background (in which an important background factor is parental education). In one of his tables he shows, for instance, how the number of composers and compositions recognized by interviewees at different educational levels is dependent on their social background. Let us examine a small section of this table, which shows the number of compositions that people with the highest level of academic education recognized, classified by class of origin (see Table 4.2).

Social background is clearly a relevant factor in this analysis, but not a highly significant one. Indeed Bourdieu points out that the importance of social background declines as one moves towards the more 'legitimate' areas of culture. This is understandable in the sense that knowledge in the core areas of the arts yields the greatest 'profits', while a low level of knowledge and skills in these areas will cause the greatest embarrassment.

Table 4.2   **Number of compositions known among people at highest educational level by class of origin (percentage)**

| Class of origin | Number of works known | | | |
	0–2	3–6	7–11	12+
Working	0	7.0	66.5	26.5
Middle	0	22.0	49.0	29.0
Upper	8.0	13.5	38.5	40.0

Source: Bourdieu 1984, 64

Table 4.3 Furniture purchases among people with highest educational level by social origin (percentage of respondents who bought their furniture from each source)

Class of origin	Department store	Specialized shop	Flea market	Auction	Antique-dealer
Working and middle	21.5	46.5	32.0	21.5	43.0
Upper	18.0	29.0	8.0	13.0	60.5

Source: Bourdieu 1984, 78

This is why a conscious effort is needed to increase one's knowledge of the arts. Indeed differences related to social background tend to be more pronounced in the case of the less significant and more private areas of taste. This can be seen for instance when we study where people in different social classes go shopping for their furniture (see Table 4.3).

Bourdieu's study goes to show, most brilliantly so, that a quantitative analysis does not have to be an unimaginative exercise of testing hypotheses. At the same time, however, his case does draw our attention to some of the limitations of the survey method. Bourdieu's theory, which he has applied to the study of various aspects of social life, is not in fact a product of statistical analysis. He worked out his theory before he entered sociology, when he was using the methods of anthropological fieldwork in a study of an Algerian village.

By means of survey analysis it is quite difficult to develop fresh perspectives or to come up with new ways of interpreting the researched phenomena. This is because of the inherent requirements of the method. The researchers must have a reasonably clear idea of the hypotheses they want to test and the preset responses they will set out before the interviews are even started. The researcher who is planning to do a social survey may not yet know the results of the study, but he or she will need to know the broad framework within which the statistical evidence will be analysed. At worst, a social survey consists in nothing else than a testing of hypotheses, the aim of which is not to discover anything new but to prove something that has already been discovered, or to produce different sorts of numerical data and distributions.

Explaining differences

The quantifying method is based above all on explaining *differences* between values obtained for different units of analysis. The units of analysis may be individuals or larger groups of people, such as populations of different statistical areas or countries; or they may be different eras or cultural products, such as different newspapers. However, the principle is always the same: the statistical analysis is based on a search for statistical regularities in the way that the values of different variables are related to each other. What is *common* to all units of analysis does not, in the context of quantitative research, provide any clues with regard to the phenomena that are to be explained; instead it is excluded, by definition, from the methodological means. What is common to all subjects belongs to the determinants of the population, and (as we saw earlier) the boundaries of the population determine the boundaries for the generalizations drawn from the study.

However, the basic idea of the quantifying method – to proceed from an explanation of individual differences and historical or temporal variation to a generic model of explanation – is used as an element in almost all scientific research. This is the case, for instance, in historical research, where the focal concern is with the logic of changes over time. The same applies to comparative cultural anthropology, which is concerned to study humans as cultural creatures and to demonstrate the cultural embeddedness of different customs and thought-models through comparisons of the ways of life of different peoples.

CHAPTER 5

ETHNOGRAPHIC RESEARCH

The ethnographic research method has its origins in the age of exploration, which saw many European adventurers returning from their travels around the world with detailed accounts of what they had seen. One of the first explorers to report on the popular customs of foreign cultures was Marco Polo, who around 1275 presented an interesting account of Kublai Khan's empire in Peking. By the beginning of the nineteenth century, early anthropologists in Europe had enough material to explore the nature of human societies on a global scale (Garbarino 1983, 9).

It is easy to understand that the natives (as they would have been called) in these far-flung countries and their peculiar behaviour aroused the interest and curiosity of Western travellers. It was above all the *difference* of these people that caught their attention, those aspects of the behaviour and social life of the indigenous people that differed from European customs and beliefs. Indeed the anthropological research that was inspired in the nineteenth century by these descriptions has sometimes been described as the study of the *other*.

The identification and explanation of differences (between Europeans and native people, between tribes on different continents and in different regions), i.e. comparison, was also central to the ethnographic research tradition that was inspired by the accounts of travellers, and later by the accounts of missionaries and colonists. The same goes for quantitative social research. However, the level of abstraction and the meaning of the distinctions made is completely different in ethnography than in statistical social research. Ethnography has paid far less attention than quantitative research to internal differences within foreign cultures, either at the individual or at the group level. And even where ethnography has drawn attention to these kinds of differences, they have not had the same function as in the methods of survey research where differences are examined with a view to providing universal explanations. Differences between male and female behaviour, for instance, are regarded as evidence of the existence of a set of cultural norms and rules on what are regarded as male and female roles. While the survey researcher is concerned to identify the individual, even within small samples, on the basis of the values that this individual has obtained on different variables, the ethnographer will describe the distinctive characteristics of a whole culture by comparing those characteristics with the 'Western' way of thinking.

This methodological difference between quantitative and ethnographic research can be traced back to the need in Europe for ethnographic information, which further stimulated the interest in foreign peoples. European colonialism had a decisive impact in this regard. The fleets that set sail from the European centres were on a mission not only to bring back raw materials, spices and gold, but also to bring the indigenous peoples under colonial rule. For both these purposes it was essential to have information about local customs and ways of thinking. These information needs, however, were still quite adequately met by basic, general knowledge; no one needed to know about individual differences. Neither did colonial governments (unlike state apparatuses in modern European societies) have any systems in place to monitor and control individuals. Colonial rule was in essence a military exercise of physical superiority.

The view that 'primitive' society was a uniform, homogeneous collectivity that allowed for no real individual differences was grounded in the European interest in knowledge. However, the societies and native cultures that travellers discovered on other continents did in fact differ from each other, often fundamentally so. In these societies old institutional structures were still intact, they had not been superseded by a social division of labour based on monetary exchange and its forceful effects on people's living conditions. This is another reason why the quantitative method was so poorly suited to the study of native cultures.

These distinctive features of anthropological research still apply to ethnography today. Ethnographic research is most typically a study of the 'other', focusing on a collectivity or group of people rather than taking a set of variables and analysing the group into a sample of discrete individuals. Unlike quantitative social research, which aims to explain differences with a view to making empirical generalizations and uncovering sociological laws, the ethnographic method is concerned with what the subjects are thought to share in common (cf. Ragin 1994, 86, *passim*). Even when ethnographically oriented qualitative researchers collect many instances of the phenomena under study, and even though they have a keen eye on, for instance, individuals' different roles or strategies in a 'meaning community', the idea is to relate such observations to what actors share in common. Different theoretical traditions have slightly different names for this common element: in addition to the most commonly used concept of culture, scholars may, for instance, talk about the collective consciousness, intersubjectivity or collective subjectivity. All ethnographic research, however, shares the same objective of laying bare, from within, the logic that informs and organizes the collectivity's life and way of thinking. In one way or another, its interest has been with questions related to the difference, to the otherness of the collectivity or group of people concerned. Over the past decades and centuries, the work that has been done within this tradition has involved exploration, adventures to find out more about the life of peoples, groups and collectivities in response to information needs stemming from administrative or social problems.

Participant observation

The rules of the ethnographic method took shape in the 1920s. A major influence was Bronislaw Malinowski's *Argonauts of the Western Pacific*, published in 1922. In the Introduction to his book, Malinowski explains at some length his fieldwork methods – and in doing so unwittingly lays down the guidelines for ethnographic research that have been followed up until the present day.

Malinowski, who took his doctorate in mathematics and physics, claims there is no reason why anthropology should not follow the same rigorous criteria of scientific work as are applied in the natural sciences. One of these criteria is *validity*, which means that in an experimental setting the instruments used to measure different phenomena should measure exactly what they are supposed to measure. The most basic requirement of validity, Malinowski asserts, is that the researcher explains how the material has been collected and the results arrived at:

> No one would dream of making an experimental contribution to physical or chemical science, without giving a detailed account of all the arrangements of the experiments; an exact description of the apparatus used; of the manner in which the observations were conducted; of their number; of the length of time devoted to them, and of the degree of approximation with which each measurement was made. In less exact sciences, as in biology or geology, this cannot be done as rigorously, but every student will do his best to bring home to the reader all the conditions in which the experiment or the observations were made. In Ethnography, where a candid account of such data is perhaps even more necessary, it has unfortunately in the past not always been supplied with sufficient generosity, and many writers do not ply the full searchlight of methodic sincerity, as they move among their facts but produce them before us out of complete obscurity. (Malinowski 1961, 2–3)

A detailed account of the research process, Malinowski continues, allows the reader better to assess which factors and circumstances may have influenced the reported events and situations as well as what the informants have said – and accordingly to decide whether the conclusions drawn from the material are reliable. Malinowski has the same thing in mind when he advises the ethnographer to spend enough time with the people under investigation. This way the ethnographer's presence will not influence the reality being studied:

> It must be remembered that the natives saw me constantly every day, they ceased to be interested or alarmed, or made self-conscious by my presence, and I ceased to be a disturbing element in the tribal life which I was to study, altering it by my very approach, as always happens with a new-comer to every savage community. (ibid., 7–8)

Malinowski's third validity rule is that theories and interpretations must be kept strictly apart from direct observations
and informant statements. The readers must have sufficient
material – descriptions as well as statistical and other background information – so that they can make a fair assessment of
the validity of the ethnographer's interpretations.

The aim of ethnographic research, according to Malinowski,
is to unravel, 'from within', the internal logic of the behaviour
and ways of thinking that are characteristic of the culture
concerned. The ethnographer should describe the world and
social reality as they present themselves from the point of view
of the people studied. '[The] goal is, briefly, to grasp the native's
point of view, his relation to life, to realize *his* vision of *his*
world' (ibid., 25).

In the process of uncovering the inner logic of what initially
appears as a strange way of life, ethnographic research also
brings order to the fragmented, seemingly irrational reality. It
shows that the anthropologist's 'savages' do not in fact rely on
their animal instincts but are human beings whose life is
governed by law, morals and aesthetic views.

This is where an independent ethnographic method has its
chance. If there is an inner logic to all the disorder and
confusion that we see on the surface of social life, ethnographers should be able to uncover that logic. To prove that
there is a logic to the behaviour and the ways of thinking in the
culture concerned, ethnographers will collect background data
on genealogies, kinship terms and demography; they will collect typical narratives, utterances, proverbs and other items of
folklore; they will report on everyday life, different customs,
patterns of behaviour; they will describe ceremonial as well as
everyday situations; and they will interview people, take notes
of informants' accounts and interpretations of the meaning and
purpose of different things and different customs. The purpose
of all this is to gain a broad, comprehensive picture of all
aspects of the culture in question. Ethnographers should never
focus their view on a single, narrow research problem and make
observations only of what is directly related to the subject of the
study.

It follows from this concern with the broader picture that
ethnographers are interested in their informants not as individuals, but as individual representatives of their culture. As

Malinowski says, the ethnographer's concern is to study stereo-typed manners of thinking and feeling. This does not mean to say that individuals are pushed aside as uninteresting and trivial; it is simply that ethnographers should use their research material to identify the particular context, the basic dimensions and outlook on the world, within which local customs and ways of thinking can be understood by people coming from a different cultural background. Made aware of these stereotyped ways of thinking and feeling, the reader should no longer make judgements of what may seem peculiar behaviour on the basis of a set of criteria that are not applicable to this culture:

> The social and cultural environment in which they move forces them to think and feel in a definite manner. Thus, a man who lives in a polyandrous community cannot experience the same feelings of jealousy, as a strict monogynist, though he might have the elements of them. (ibid., 23)

One might be tempted to think of ethnographic research and ethnography simply in terms of making observations about the community's way of life and asking people questions about their customs. Malinowski makes it clear this is not the case. The fact that there exists an inner logic which governs the life of a people does not mean to say that the ethnographer's job consists simply of collecting informant accounts and organizing those accounts. Ethnography does not consist simply of a foreign people or community talking about their life and their beliefs to the scientific community and, through the ethno-grapher, to the reading audience. This is because the internal logic of the culture is not based on any conscious pattern of behaviour or strategy. Rather, that logic, the essence of the culture, lies in the fundamental assumptions about the nature of reality which are handed down from generation to generation and which provide the foundation for all communication and interaction among the members of the community. People are not aware of these assumptions, indeed they are not regarded as *assumptions* or beliefs in the first place; they simply are there, they are facts of life. To regard these assumptions as religious beliefs would require an ability to imagine that there are other ways in which to look at life and reality. On the other hand, many basic assumptions which guide people's behaviour are not talked about because they are taken for granted, even though they are not made explicit:

> The regularities in native institutions are an automatic result of the interaction of the mental forces of tradition, and of the material conditions of environment. Exactly as a humble member of any modern institution, whether it be the state, or the church, or the army, is *of* it and *in* it, but has no vision of the resulting integral action of the whole, still less could furnish any account of its organisation, so it would be futile to attempt questioning a native in abstract, sociological terms. (ibid., 11–12)

It is for this reason that, as Malinowski says, the ethnographer cannot extract an explanation directly from the interview; the interview can merely provide clues about the anatomy of the culture. Informants may be asked to offer comments on concrete situations, they may be asked to say what they think about something that has happened, to explain their view. All of this material can be used with the ethnographer's descriptions and the background information he or she has collected as evidence in the search for a solution to the enigma. In other words, ethnography proceeds along the same path as detective stories where the clues have to be organized so that they do not conflict with each other.

From this point of view what Malinowski says about the meaning of theory is understandable. On the one hand, he points out that theory is all-important to the ethnographer, that the fieldworker relies entirely on inspiration from theory. On the other hand, he says it is essential that theory and theorizing are kept strictly apart from observations. Theoretical ideas, for Malinowski, are general models on the basis of which the ethnographer can try to organize the material into a coherent, logical whole. Theory, for its part, is an inspiration for fieldwork, for the collection of material, in two ways. Firstly, theories help to draw the observer's attention to things that would pass unnoticed to anyone with a neutral, normal attitude. Secondly, theories may point at interpretations of the material that one might otherwise never think of. However, every explanation must always be tested against the hard empirical facts.

This could be compared to the example we gave in Chapter 3 where Holmes was wondering about the dog that did not bark.

The reason why Holmes latched onto this point, the framework for his observations, was the knowledge that a guard dog should be expected to bark if a stranger enters the dog's territory. However, as it turned out, this knowledge did not directly contribute to the solution of the case.

Sometimes, of course, a particular theory of social interaction may provide the foundations for the whole explanation. For instance, the idea that people's behavioural patterns can be better explained if we have adequate knowledge about the community's cultural traditions and its current living conditions provides such a framework. However, it is merely a general model which draws our attention to the facts mentioned. A theoretical framework should not deductively determine the contents of the observations made. Malinowski says that theories should *broaden* our horizons, not narrow them down, by bringing in new, preconceived ideas.

This is reflected in Malinowski's description of fieldwork as a dialectical process. Every now and then the ethnographer should pause to review and check the empirical facts that have been collected against his or her theoretical ideas, to test what sort of outline could be constructed on the basis of these facts. Equipped with the experience from this 'interim report' – that is, an attempt to solve the case – the ethnographer can go back out in the field to collect more material which will help to test the validity of the initial constructive attempts. If the new material shows that those attempts were all wrong, the ethnographer has to try to find new models and test them.

Observant participation

If Malinowski's ethnographic method is compared with more recent texts on the techniques, methods and theoretical foundations of fieldwork, the biggest difference lies perhaps in the epistemological perspective advocated by later theorists and fieldworkers. Although Malinowski's method represents participant observation, the emphasis is clearly on exact *observation*.

Having said that, it must of course be admitted that Malinowski's approach does contain the seeds of sensitive participation as well: 'Again, in this type of work, it is good for the Ethnographer sometimes to put aside camera, note book and pencil, and to join in himself in what is going on' (ibid., 21). Malinowski says that participation helps the ethnographer get a better 'feel' for what is 'good' or what is 'bad' behaviour according to local criteria. However, unlike more recent authors and theorists, he does not construct out of 'bad' or 'wrong' behaviour a specific method of data collection, nor does he in any other way indicate that one way of obtaining 'clues' is to look at the reactions caused by the ethnographer's interference in the course of events. Malinowski wants to remain in the background, arguing that once the ethnographer has spent enough time with the natives, they will no longer be bothered, i.e. that the ethnographer's presence will no longer influence the phenomenon that is being studied. The argument is the same as the natural scientist's, that the measuring device, in this case the researcher's personality, has not influenced the results of the measurement.

The situation is different in a number of more recent methodic ideas and epistemological viewpoints. In ethno-methodology, for instance, researchers have aimed specifically to lay bare the invisible rules and presumptions that govern our everyday life by looking at what happens when people break these rules and presumptions. In an ethnomethodological study you might, for instance, want to know what happens when someone greets you by saying 'How are you?', and you reply by saying that that depends on whether the question refers to your health, your financial situation, success at school, peace of mind or something else (Garfinkel 1984, 44). In other words the idea of ethnomethodology is to explore and to make visible the taken-for-granted rules of interpretation that people use in their everyday life as well as the collectively shared assumptions on the basis of which we make sense of different interaction situations. The rules and frames of interpretation not only help to make sense of different interaction situations, they also *produce* these situations.

People researching foreign cultures and their unwritten rules do not have to make any special effort to break these rules; they will do so unwittingly. However, the more recent literature on the ethnographic method does not consider this a serious problem, as something that attracts needless attention to the researcher and in this way disturbs the 'natural everyday life' that is being observed. On the contrary, it has been pointed out that it is precisely the 'horizon of taken-for-granted everyday practices' that makes possible ethnography of a foreign culture or sphere of life. Since the researcher's own way of life is based on various taken-for-granted practices, new situations will continue to emerge in the course of fieldwork where the researcher either does not understand or does not accept what is happening. The researcher may feel threatened, or that the role of 'researcher' is inadequate, or that it is dishonest. Willis (1978) points out that these kinds of clashes between two subjective meaning-constructs are particularly valuable because they make visible different kinds of world-views.

Ethnographic research is always fundamentally about comparing two different world-views. It starts out from specific aspects in the subjects' way of life which 'deviate' from the corresponding aspects in the researcher's way of life. These differences prompt the researcher to question the presumptions of his or her own model. This, in turn, provides clues as to what kind of questions the researcher could ask of the subjects and what kind of aspects he or she could focus on in observing the group. In the process of talking with the group, observing the group and making constructive attempts, the researcher gains a deeper understanding not only of the way of life of the group studied, but also of the obscure presumptions that lie behind his or her own world-view.

A similar process occurs among the subjects. Informants must also perform a translation operation from one cultural domain to another, take distance from their own culture and explain its features in a language that the researcher and the subject can both understand. Initially the researcher and the informant are on two different continents, trying to find a ford where they could make the crossing and get together. Slowly, the people involved in the study begin to find common ground and a ridge begins to form between the two cultures so that the crossing can safely be made on foot. This is how Paul Rabinow (1977, 119) puts it:

> Whenever an anthropologist enters a culture, he trains people to objectify their life-world to him. Within all cultures, of course, there is already objectification and self-reflection. But this explicit self-

conscious translation into an external medium is rare. The anthropologist creates a doubling of consciousness.

Anthropological analysis, Rabinow says, must take account of two things. Firstly, we ourselves are always historically situated, which is apparent in the questions we ask and in the way in which we seek to understand and experience the world. Secondly, what we receive from our informants are interpretations, which are equally mediated by history and culture.

During the research process both the researcher and the informant have to take distance from their respective spheres of life and from their customs, to explain them from a new perspective, which has to be constructed out of the elements offered by the other party. Both the researcher and the informant move increasingly in a border zone in-between two cultures, which is no easy task (Rabinow 1977, 39).

The situation is different in normal everyday life. People who live and work in their own culture do not need to pay any attention to the taken-for-granted practices of that culture. They are instead preoccupied by the things they have to do at home or at work, by the problems they have to address today. In so far as their everyday life goes more or less smoothly and normally, people will assume that everyone else around them shares the same basic assumptions about social reality and about what is happening and the meanings of different events. This kind of web of meanings that underlies all cultures allows actors to live their lives from day to day and hour to hour without having to reconstruct their social relations on the basis of trivial little clues, or without having to engage in a constant debate on semantics. In this sense everyday consciousness is 'thin'; it is loosely articulated, it is largely taken for granted (Rabinow 1977, 30).

If common sense is 'thin', the ethnographer's aim should be to produce a 'thick description' (Geertz 1973), an analysis which only seems to be possible by comparing the life-world studied with a different, foreign life-world. This is one of the reasons why research which uses the ethnographic method is a study of the 'other', the foreign.

But what happens when social scientists are concerned to study their own society, the culture they breathe every day? Is ethnographic research, in this situation, impossible; or does it simply become thinner as the researchers come closer to their own sphere of life?

This does not have to be the case, for two reasons. First of all, modern society is not so static and everyday life is accordingly not so smooth and unproblematic that people could manage without every now and then reflecting on and readjusting their self-evident assumptions. It was precisely the constant changes in the social structure which meant that people had to throw overboard their accustomed routines and ways of thinking that stimulated the sociological imagination in the general population. The changes did not stop with the Industrial Revolution and the breakthrough of capitalism; on the contrary, smaller and greater structural changes have continued to follow at an accelerating rate. Each generation must for its part study its living conditions and in that context form its own notion of a good and meaningful life. This is seen in the rise of so-called youth cultures especially after the Second World War: it is the new generation that enters social life as independent individuals who have to resolve the contradictions between the values they have inherited from their parents and the new, changing living conditions. In this light it is no surprise that the ethnographic method has been used so widely and so successfully in the study of youth cultures (e.g. Hall and Jefferson 1975; Hebdige, 1979; Mungham and Pearson 1976; Willis 1977, 1978). Young people *are* an 'other' culture, and they are in a situation which allows them to look upon their life from the outside, to move with ease, as good informants will, in the border zone between two cultures.

A second reason why ethnographic research can be used in the study of one's own culture is provided by the role of *theory*, as highlighted earlier by Malinowski. When the clues for the process of ethnographic deduction are produced in a clash of two cultures, theory serves as a kind of third position, a vantage-point from which researchers can make their observations. The role of theory could be compared to a Japanese person who is reading an ethnographic analysis by an American anthropologist of an African tribe. The Japanese readers, against their own cultural background, turn their attention to points that the American has missed in his or her study of Africans. The ethnographic report increases our awareness of the presumptions hidden within the cultures of both the subject and the ethnographer, but it may easily ignore those basic assumptions about the world that both Americans and Africans take for granted. This is where theory is needed.

The theoretical framework is always broader than the border zone based on explaining the differences between two cultures, because it (ideally) represents all the accumulated knowledge about all known cultures. This is why researchers can also analyse their own way of life, taking distance from it through the theoretical framework.

All anthropological theories boil down, in effect, to one and the same thing: they are succinct empirical generalizations about the nature of human interaction. Unlike theories in clinical medicine or any other natural science, they do not set deterministic models which predict future events, instead they try to explain phenomena that have already happened. Nonetheless it is important that anthropological theories retain their value so that they can be used to explain future realities that as yet have not been explored. Although ethnographic research is concerned to explain concrete events, 'the theoretical framework in terms of which such an interpretation is made must be capable of continuing to yield defensible interpretations as new social phenomena swim into view', as Geertz (1973, 26–27) describes the principle.

However, this is not to say that comparative ethnographic research necessarily produces or tries to produce universal generalizations of humans as natural creatures. Although a good anthropological theory should provide the starting-point for a convincing explanation for phenomena occurring in any culture we know, it is in the spirit of the ethnographic method to suggest that all of the cultures known in the world today represent little more than a faint shimmer of the full potential of the human species, the inventiveness of people and all the forms that human society in principle could assume. Even so, a knowledge of cultural differences and cultural diversity is of primary importance because ethnographic research broadens our horizons. To paraphrase Wittgenstein: the boundaries of the cultures we know constitute the boundaries of our world.

From the working-class question to youth cultures

The history of ethnographic research in Western countries clearly illustrates that the ethnographic method is concerned to study groups and collectivities who are thought to share the same or similar world-views and life-styles. This has had two implications. On the one hand, in our individualizing society, researchers have moved on to a level of abstraction where individual differences are of secondary importance compared with common, shared features. On the other hand, the natural boundaries of the method have forced researchers to turn their attention to ever smaller groups within a society which is increasingly fragmented into separate individuals or at least into private households. As a consequence it has been difficult for researchers to demonstrate that their results have any broader relevance in society.

In social research concerned with modern societies, the ethnographic tradition started in England with Friedrich Engels, who was the first scholar to go out and see the slums where the working classes lived in the major industrial centres of Yorkshire and Lancashire and all over the British Isles: London, Dublin, Edinburgh, Glasgow, Liverpool, Bristol. Engels's accounts of all the poverty and destitution he saw in the squalid streets and back alleys of these slums were highly detailed and emotionally charged.

Engels's contribution to the development of the ethnographic method in this line of research was that he was the first to recognize the need and importance of going out to see for oneself what was happening and to report on one's findings in a detailed field diary. This was motivated not only by Engels's own personal curiosity, but also by his view that in most cities the working-class quarters had been systematically hidden behind the clean high-street façades, out of reach and out of sight of the bourgeoisie and the middle classes (Engels 1987 [1845], 86).

Engels was followed by a succession of researchers and philanthropists who applied the methods of ethnography to studying the 'working-class question'. One name that deserves separate mention is Henry Mayhew, a journalist who went out to explore the slums of Manchester just a few years after Engels.

Unlike Engels, who by way of statistical analyses demonstrated that the individual experiences of poverty were due, in the last instance, to social conditions of capitalism, Mayhew drew attention to the individuals he met in these slums, to their distinctive ways of thinking and behaviours. In other words, he was more in line with the principles of the ethnographic method in that he focused on cultural forms.

However, Mayhew's methodic solutions clearly highlighted the problems that are involved in a study of the people of a whole slum as a single collectivity. Rather than trying to find something that all these people shared in common, Mayhew opted for the method of classification. He divided the poor, firstly, into honest and dishonest people, and then further classified honest people into two categories, namely striving and disabled. This yielded a classification according to which there are poor people who wish to work, poor people who are unable to work and poor people who do not want to work. This classification became the basis of organization for the remainder of the studies of the London poor (Kent 1981, 44).

The interesting thing about Mayhew is that he has one foot in ethnographic and one foot in quantitative social research: on the one hand, he is interested in finding individual differences, in making classifications, which points at the tradition of statistical social research; on the other hand, he is also concerned with the individual's motives and strategies of action, which points in the direction of *Verstehen*: that is, interpretive sociology and particularly the concept of ideal-type that was later proposed by Max Weber.

In the United States the development of ethnographic research on modern society has followed largely the same general pattern as the European tradition of urban ethnography, which started from the study of the working-class question. In particular, mention must be made of the Chicago School and its studies into the subcultures of ethnic minorities in major US cities. Since it started in the 1920s the school's focal concern was with urbanization: with how cities, these structures that people had shaped, themselves shape people (Park et al. 1967). The method of participant observation was in active use within the Chicago School: Frederick Thrasher (1960), for instance, carried out a survey of the youth gangs of Chicago. Methods of fieldwork were developed especially by William Foote Whyte, a later student of the Chicago School, in his study *Street Corner Society* (1981 [1943]), which examined the social structure of slums occupied by Italian Americans. He was also later to discuss his methods of social study (Whyte 1984).

The Chicago School is a particularly interesting case in that it inspired widespread interest in young people and the culture of the gang and youth subcultures. This shift is understandable, for two reasons. Firstly, ethnographic research has traditionally taken an interest in groups and collectivities which for one reason or another have been considered problematic and whose way of life has remained more or less obscure in the absence of anything other than numerical data. Young people, and particularly the youth of ethnic minorities in working-class or lower status positions, have emerged as a specific social problem since the Second World War; the 'working-class question' has turned into the 'youth question'. Secondly, youth gangs are quite a rarity in modern society in that there remain very few groups here which form spontaneously: the ethnographic method is ideally suited to studying such groups.

From this point of view it is understandable that the British tradition of ethnographic research has also concentrated on studying working-class culture and working-class youth culture. The tradition started with Richard Hoggart's (1957) study *The Uses of Literacy*, in which Hoggart turned his attention away from serious, high-brow literature and applied his research tools to the study of everyday life and light entertainment. Although Hoggart was a founding figure and the first director of Birmingham's Centre for Contemporary Cultural Studies, the culturalist line of ethnographic research was particularly influenced by the later developments of the Birmingham School, which is famous for its studies of working-class culture and youth subcultures (e.g. Clarke et al. 1979; Hall and Jefferson 1975; Willis 1977, 1978). Its research interests were inspired by growing public concern, echoed by government authorities, about racism in Britain and about the growth of football hooliganism on the terraces, for example. The ethnographic studies by the Birmingham School highlighted the connections of these trends with the economy. And, in line with the ethnographic tradition, they showed that the way of life of youth gangs, even those involved in criminal activities, is organized by its own internal logic.

Towards New Ethnography

In recent years the division of labour between anthropologists studying the distant 'exotic' others and sociologists studying their 'own' culture or subcultures has become more and more blurred. Owing to economic developments of post-colonialism, large-scale migration has made many countries and practically all major cities multicultural, with different 'ethnic' groups living next to or mixed with each other. At the same time modern mass media and increasingly efficient networks of communication mix world cultures, enhancing both homogenization and new differentiations along the lines of ethnicity, gender, socio-economic position and sexual orientation, for instance. These developments are said to make individuals increasingly self-reflexive about who they are. A romanticist view of intact 'native cultures', waiting to be observed and captured in ethnographic reports, is irreversibly *passé*. When, for instance, an anthropologist born in Trinidad and trained in the United States goes back to his or her country of origin to do fieldwork (Stewart 1989), who are 'us' and who are the 'other'?

This does not mean to say that ethnography is in crisis. On the contrary, increasingly often not only anthropologists but also sociologists, media researchers and representatives of many other disciplines describe their approach as 'ethnographic'. One even talks about an interdisciplinary 'ethnographic turn'. However, we could talk about a crisis of representation and about a problematization of the notion of the 'field' or location in present-day ethnographic research.

The crisis of representation refers to the simple point made in the recent discussion that apart from participant observation, ethnography is writing; that is what anthropologists – and social scientists – do (Geertz 1973, 1988). As a form of writing, ethnography can be called fiction in the sense of 'something made or fashioned', which is what the word's Latin root *fingere* means (Clifford and Marcus 1986, 6). This does not imply that ethnographies are false descriptions of cultures or social milieux, but it does draw attention to the fact that ethnographic writing is determined and conditioned contextually, rhetorically, institutionally, generically, politically and historically. As was pointed out in the previous section, an ethnographic report wants to make sense of an 'other culture' to its readership, and that is why it is necessarily conditioned by the differences and similarities between the described culture and that of the implied readership. As much as it makes a strange 'other' look familiar and understandable, it contributes to making the familiar look strange, less self-evident, and from the viewpoint of the readers that may in fact be its main function. To create before the eyes of an implied reader a vivid picture of an 'other', the ethnographer needs to give a fairly detailed description of an unfamiliar social milieu, but that can only be achieved by resorting to words and tropes with which the implied reader is familiar. To succeed, the author also has to take into account the changing expressive conventions by which the report's reception is conditioned. Like it or not, the ethnographer places him- or herself in a particular position in relation to the objects and readership of the study. There is no universal divine position from which to write equally to all human beings.

The problematization of the 'field' in ethnographic 'fieldwork' is related to the same issue (Gupta and Ferguson 1997). The notion of the field carries within it an image of an ethnographer going out to a particular field site, spending a considerable amount of time studying the 'local' people, and returning home to write up an ethnographic report. This archetypal image includes a radical separation of 'the field' from 'home'. Secondly, it prioritizes knowledge of a 'local setting', an object of knowledge which can be defined geographically and studied by means of participant observation. Thirdly, it constructs an anthropological 'self' against which anthropology sets its 'others' (Gupta and Ferguson 1997, 12–18).

This archetypal image of the field fits poorly with much of contemporary ethnography. For one thing, anthropologists are increasingly aware of the fact that 'culture areas' are always social constructions, dependent on the anthropologists' (funding) providing home countries' strategic and geopolitical strategies. For instance, a few years ago there was an effort in American anthropology to carve out a new area, 'Inner Asia', which would be distinct from Eastern Europe and Soviet studies, on the one hand, and the Middle East and China, on the other. It was motivated by the concern with Afghanistan and fears of a possible ascendance of 'Islamic republics' in the regions adjacent to what was then the Soviet Union (Gupta and Ferguson 1997, 9). Secondly, several 'groups' or 'communities' studied in complex societies do not reside in any particular site or location; they are instead 'virtual communities', theoretical constructs created by the researcher. For instance, the audience of a film or the fans of a rock group can be approached as one or more 'interpretive communities' and shown to inhabit a set amount of discourses within which the cultural product is received and consumed, but this does not take place in a particular 'field site'. In media studies, for instance, Allor (1988), Grossberg (1988) and Radway (1988) have emphasized that no such thing as the 'audience' really exists out there; one must bear in mind that audience is, first and foremost, a discursive construct produced by a particular analytic gaze. As Grossberg (1988, 386) puts it, 'media audiences are shifting constellations, located within varying multiple discourses which are never entirely outside of the media discourse themselves'.

The very notion of 'culture', however it is defined, is itself a similar social construction. There is no easy way to sift out one culture from another.

To problematize ethnography in the ways outlined above does not, however, mean that we should give up doing ethnographic studies and participant observation altogether. To get a grasp of social and cultural phenomena it is in any case often useful to conduct an extensive study of a 'local' setting. It is only that we should avoid drawing naturalist and romanticist conclusions about the results. The ethnographic gaze will inevitably contribute to the production of the objects it sets out to describe and analyse in the first place. Whether we like it or not, by describing and analysing a social milieu we will also be taking part in the ceaseless public redefinition and self-reflection of social realities. In effect, doing ethnography is no more and no less than a form of cultural critique (Marcus and Fischer 1986).

The presumptions of the ethnographic method

The ethnographic method stands or falls with one single presumption: the ethnographer proceeds from the assumption that the people, the subjects of the study, share something in common. Typically, this will be a culture or shared world-view, the same kind of outlook on life or way of interpreting reality, or the same set of frames or discourses within which to discuss their divergent viewpoints. It follows that the challenge for ethnographic research is to submit a viable theory of the structures of whatever it is that the subjects share in common. Ethnography abstracts from the individual features of the people in the group that is being studied.

This presumption can be compared to the situation where a detective is sifting through clues on the basis of the assumption that a crime has really happened. If there is no chain of events that needs explaining, then even the most interesting facts have no relevance because they are not connected. Likewise, if the members of the 'group' or 'collectivity' studied have nothing in common at the level where the ethnographer is trying to construct a shared structure of reality for them, the results of the study will amount to nothing more than imagination.

This basic methodological presumption of ethnographic research has caused a host of problems as research attention has turned towards the increasingly individualized society of the present day. These problems are, firstly, of a concrete nature: it is more and more difficult today to find coherent, clear-cut collectivities and to find informants who could say how 'we' live and how 'we' think, because modern individuals quite simply do not really identify themselves with any specific group, at least not strongly enough to speak for them as 'us'. As a consequence, classical ethnographic research in modern societies has turned more and more often to studying ever smaller groups. There is also an ethical side to the problem. Although the study of small groups related to people's private life (e.g. family) may seem the only possible way to apply the ethnographic method to an analysis of a given present-day phenomenon, it is hard to imagine how we could justify a study of people's intimate private life which uses the method of participant observation. The problem is also theoretical, touching on the reliability of the results. Modern people may belong to several small, like-minded groups. However, it is difficult to define the level of abstraction at which it is justified to talk about features that individuals share in common. What is more, some of the individual's reference groups may be entirely imaginary: for instance, someone may consider themselves a typical Capricorn. Part of this problem has to do with the generalizability of observations and conclusions. If it is difficult to demarcate the collectivity, then it is accordingly difficult to say to whom the results apply, or what the observations about a small group say about society at large.

The different kinds of theoretical models applied in ethnographic research may be seen as ways of resolving these problems. Max Weber's (1978 [1922]) programme of interpretive sociology is one example of this kind of model. Weber shifts the emphasis away from the community level to the individual level by defining different types of social action. He makes a distinction between instrumentally rational, value-rational, affectual and traditional action. The methodic idea behind this classification is that since the social actions of people cannot be explained as expressions of one single, collective thought-world, different phenomena and the actions of different groups are best explained by reference to different types of action. However, the classification does not mean that people are slotted into different groups accordingly, because Weber regards these four types of action as 'superempirical' ideal-types: it would be very unusual, he says, to find concrete cases of action which were oriented only in one or another of these ways. Weber's model is thus at once an attempt to resolve the problem of generalizability: he makes the statistical connections between things understandable through these four types of action.

Ethnomethodological ethnography is an example of a different kind of solution. Here, we would try not to make any assumptions about people's meaning-worlds. Rather, the focal concern is with concrete, perceivable, incarnate social actions through which actors produce everyday situations and practices and within which they are capable of acting. Ethnomethodology is concerned to investigate how social facts are produced in everyday situations of interaction. Ethnomethodology is not concerned to find out what people 'mean' or what they 'think' while they are acting, but to study the methods and the rules of interpretation on the basis of which people draw conclusions about each other's thoughts and intentions (Garfinkel 1984). In other words, whatever it is that these subjects share in common is uncovered at the level of these rules of interpretation.

CHAPTER 6

OBSERVER OR PARTICIPANT?

The 1930s marked the dawn of a new era in both detective stories and social research. The question that now commanded the attention of different schools of thought was the historical, social and institutional contingency of research and the individual researcher. The argument went beyond the point that had been made in the ethnographic tradition, i.e. that the group or collectivity studied would necessarily be influenced by the research process; there was a growing recognition now that research was in itself an institution, a form of social action. Researchers began critically to look at themselves, the work they did, the institution they represented.

From detective stories to crime novels

In crime literature the changes started in the United States with *Black Mask* magazine, whose contributors included Dashiell Hammett and Raymond Chandler. The tradition was known for its drive to create authenticity, to take the crime back to where it really happened, the dark, shady backstreets in the big cities. There was also a background of social criticism to these stories. They described the police and the mechanisms of society exactly for what they were, i.e. as fundamentally corrupt, integral parts of the fabric of professional crime. This is how Hammett describes the police in *Red Harvest*:

> The first policeman I saw needed a shave. The second had a couple of buttons off his shabby uniform. The third stood in the centre of

the city's main intersection – Broadway and Union Street – directing traffic, with a cigar in one corner of his mouth. After that I stopped checking them up.

The relationship between the private detective and his client was also to change. Ross MacDonald, a disciple of the *Black Mask* tradition, has the following description of a meeting between his detective character and client in *Blue Hammer*:

I drove up the dark hill to Biemeyer's house feeling angry and powerless. The house was blazing with lights but entirely silent.

Biemeyer answered the door with a drink held securely in his hand. He gave the impression that the drink was holding him up. Everything else about him, shoulders and knees and face, seemed to be sagging.

'What in the hell do you want?' His voice was husky and frayed, as if he had been doing a lot of shouting.

'I'd like to have a serious talk with you, Mr Biemeyer.'

'I can translate that. You want more money.'

'Forget about the money for a change. I don't care about your money.'

His face lengthened. He had hoisted his money up the mast, and I had failed to salute it. Slowly his face came together again, wrinkling around his dark hostile eyes.

'Does that mean you won't be sending me a bill?'

I was tempted to turn my back on him and leave, perhaps taking a swing at him first. But Biemeyer and his household possessed knowledge that I had to have. And working for them gave me standing with the police that I couldn't get in any other way.

This excerpt neatly captures the setting which is so characteristic of the *Black Mask* tradition and which sets it apart from earlier detective stories of the golden age. Earlier, the characters in a detective story used to include a private detective and a number of possible suspects, sometimes police officers, but the police would always be portrayed as failures who would have no chance of ever resolving the case without the main character, the private eye. In the newly evolving crime novels, authors like Chandler and MacDonald had four different kinds of characters: the detective, the client, the police and the criminals. The (typically male) detective needs the client in order to earn a living, to get paid, but he also needs legal protection as well as the client's patronage. That is, given his high moral standards, the detective will not content himself with the specific assignment but will do anything and everything necessary to find out the truth. Also, unlike Sherlock Holmes' clients, who are decent, honest citizens who have suffered some great injustice, these new-generation clients will usually be hiring a detective in order to protect their own interests. They want to find out something that is in their own best interest; and often to cover up something else that is closely related to the matter. There are two types of police officers: those who have become involved in professional crime, and those who have retained their integrity. Although this feature clearly points at the individualistic image of society in modern crime novels, at the underlying idea that justice depends ultimately on virtuous, upright individuals, the overall picture is nonetheless one of cynical realism: crime and evil are structural, in-built features of society. The police and the judicial system are not independent of prevailing power relations, or in a position of a judge over and above those power relations, but simply pawns on the board of power relations. Whether or not justice is done will depend on the power relations and alliances between the client who has commissioned the investigation, the judicial system and organized crime, and on how the detective succeeds in manipulating those relations through his own actions and strategies. And justice is not understood here in a strictly juridical sense, because often the detective will have to break the law and refuse to tell the truth in order to defend the weak and victimized individual against criminals, against the state and often even against the client. However, even when justice wins in the end, nothing changes: victory is simply the outcome of the detective's strategic skill and good luck.

Symons (1992) regards this latest turn in the history of detective stories as so significant that he says it marks a shift from detective stories to crime novels. Since this turn, he maintains, the detective story can no longer be seen as a separate category of class B light reading; crime novels must now be accepted as an independent genre of literature. Crime novels, Symons argues, are a genre of realistic stories which take a critical view on society and which are closely interwoven with other genres of literature.

There is no doubt that this is a significant turn, but the promotion of all subsequent detective stories to 'proper' literature sheds no light on what this change was really all about. Firstly, the 'realism' of a particular genre is obviously a relative question and contingent on time. It is too simplistic to say that crime writers, in this new genre, suddenly decided to tell us what crime is 'really' about and that they can therefore be upgraded to the ranks of 'real' novelists. This radical decision must be preceded by a growing awareness among writers and among the population that detective stories are quite far removed from reality, that crime and the struggle against crime include essential features that fall outside the genre concerned. In other words: when society changes, so too do people's perceptions of 'crime', and consequently the old genre of detective stories is no longer in a position to describe the 'essential' aspects of crime. A new, more credible genre grows up that is better equipped to deal with these more essential aspects.

In American society there were two significant developments that played a major part in the change of crime stories: firstly, the growth of organized crime, particularly during Prohibition, and secondly, the growth of corruption within the police force. On a larger scale, looking at the Western world as a whole, the rise of fascism and its repressive mechanisms further reinforced new perceptions of power, the state and the judicial system. In the United States these trends in development culminated in McCarthy's witch-hunts in the 1950s, a systematic campaign involving FBI detectives to disclose what was believed to be Communist infiltration of the government. Dashiell Hammett, the *Black Mask* crime writer, was jailed in the 1950s for refusing to reveal the names of contributors to the funds of a Communist front organization (Symons 1992, 158). By this time Stalin's Great Purge in the Soviet Union had also become common knowledge. All in all the era was characterized by deep cynicism, by the end of illusions.

Critical theory

In the social sciences the harbinger of the new era was a trend which developed in the late 1920s within the Frankfurt School and which became known as critical theory. The focal theme and problem for this school of thought which grew up among German Marxists was the (im)possibility of an ultimate truth as well as the position of the intellectual who was interested in studying society. Critical theory took distance from all given truths even within Marxism and denied the authority of the Communist Party of the first socialist state, i.e. the Soviet Union, as the source of official interpretations. However, institutional independence was just a starting-point. The real driving force of the school's research effort was to be to criticize all kinds of 'truths'; the chief concern was to find a vantage-point for its criticisms. This was no easy task. The very name of this new school, i.e. 'critical theory', contains an inherent contradiction, which is addressed at different stages of the history of critical theory. Instead of advancing its own ideas of what was happening in 'reality', the strategy of critical theory was to analyse and criticize the truths submitted by others and the truths prevailing in society, to demonstrate that these were historically contingent; hence the 'critical'. On the other hand, what made this critique possible in the first place was a materialist concept of history, the view that the forms of consciousness prevailing at any given time in society are determined by the material foundations of society, specifically its modes of production. In this sense the Frankfurt School did include a positive theory of the ultimate nature of reality, or at least its critique was grounded in certain baseline assumptions with regard to the nature of reality. In this sense critical theory did not just criticize theories advocated by others, but it also included an effort to *build* theory.

This internal tension within critical theory was reflected in the positions taken by school members on *Ideology and Utopia*, Karl Mannheim's work which was published in German in 1929 and in English in 1936. It was widely agreed within the school that Mannheim had gone too far. However, there were two conflicting lines of criticism.

In his introduction to the sociology of knowledge in this book, Mannheim argues that the social contingency of all knowledge also applies to Marxism. He points out not only that the concept of ideology should be applied to refer to 'false consciousness', but that all scientific theories are inevitably shaped and influenced by the author's historical and social situation:

> There is scarcely a single intellectual position, and Marxism furnishes no exception to this rule, which has not changed through history and which even in the present does not appear in many forms. Marxism, too, has taken on many diverse appearances. It should not be too difficult for a Marxist to recognize their social basis. (Mannheim 1979 [1936], 69)

On the other hand, the 'socially unattached intelligentsia' (*freischwebende Intelligenz*) who are outside of all classes advocating and defending their interests should, Mannheim suggests, be able to break loose from positions that are historically and socially contingent by relating them to each other and to society and hence at this more general level obtain positive knowledge about reality. In other words, they can replace relativism by relationism.

Initially the critics attacked Mannheim for 'betraying' Marxism as just another ideology among others, revealing that all knowledge was conditioned upon social existence – and consequently for rejecting the Marxist distinction between real (class) consciousness and false consciousness. On the other hand, Max Horkheimer criticized Mannheim for his theory of relationism, which suggested that there existed an ultimate truth (Jay 1974, 63–64).

This question that the Frankfurt School raised with regard to the contingency of social knowledge was an important one and hard to resolve. The intellectual, the social researcher, was now increasingly recognized as a member of society and as a child of his or her time. The same observation was made by American sociologist C. Wright Mills. However, whereas the most burning issue for the Frankfurt School was the researcher's relationship to political institutions, Mills focused his attention on the impacts of the university system and institutionalized social research on the nature of the knowledge produced. The chief reason for this difference was that by the 1950s, when C. Wright Mills wrote *The Sociological Imagination* (Mills 1977 [1959]), empirical social research in the United States had already become established as a social institution with its own routines; it had become a means of control, community planning and politics. In the form of survey research, empirical social research explored and classified social problems, sought to identify what were thought to be distinct causal reasons, carried out market research to help advertise and sell products, and took part through opinion polls in political speculation.

With the growing significance of this kind of social research, the production of social knowledge had become an industrial and bureaucratic exercise; researchers had become administrators, research directors or research engineers. Since the volume of social research had increased so phenomenally, the division of labour and management in university research institutes was organized on industrial or military principles. For this to be possible it was necessary to standardize the products of the operation, i.e. the research reports. As far as methodology was concerned, researchers were now adopting the principles of what Mills described as 'abstracted empiricism': a methodology based on rules of deduction and verification that were independent of the subject-matter and the problem investigated. Research directors touted for new research projects, dictated the problems they were to address or passed them straight on from client to the research technicians, who would start up their production lines, collect and process the material and produce a report. The prescribed task for social research was now to control social problems and to predict future trends in development. Its research problems were the very same problems that managers and administrators were having at work. The input of new, fresh ideas from research into the debate on the nature of social phenomena began to dry up as more and more attention went to meeting the requirement that research results should show objective reliability. This, of course, is paradoxical in that the socio-technical knowledge used for purposes of political and economic decision-making had an increasingly central role as an extension of the administrative apparatus.

Mills' analysis of the status of social research in American society in the 1950s bears a striking resemblance to the settings we find in the crime stories of his contemporary Raymond Chandler. Both for Chandler's Philip Marlowe and for Mills the discovery of the truth remains a priority concern, but the tension of the narrative no longer comes solely from the clues that are thrown up by the narrative. The new, emerging theme is one of a balancing act between the ethical principles of the investigator who is looking for the truth, the expectations of the client who is paying the bill and providing protection, and the conditions set by the official administrative system and the police force. The solutions also have a great deal in common. Mills calls upon the researchers to use their sociological imagination, to break loose from the intellectual straitjacket of abstracted empiricism. Chandler brings private detective Philip Marlowe on to the scene, a man of honour who is not afraid and whose soul is untarnished. Relying on his skills and instincts (and helped by a measure of good luck), he manages to bring his cases to a happy ending, or least to an ethically acceptable conclusion in a world that is unlikely to become a better place for it. In other words, both Chandler and Mills believed that a careless investigator may unwittingly become a pawn in the social power game, and that if he or she is not aware of this risk he or she may be misled. The investigator was located as an agent in the complex web of power relations, and this was considered a threat to the discovery of truth and to justice being done.

This applies more generally to the themes that were raised by critical theory. The contents of social theories were subjected to ideological critique by relating them to the social standings of the people who had developed them, and social research as a whole was seen as a social institution, not only as a passive outside observer. However, these critical insights did not lead to new methodic strategies. Instead of analysing the social and historical contingency of their own thoughts and instead of working to develop new methodological solutions, critical theorists wanted to resolve the problem in a more traditional fashion by trying to step outside of history and their own position in society.

Action research

The situation is different in the case of *action research*, whose origins are often traced back to Kurt Lewin's work from the 1940s onwards. This approach is set apart from the rest of the field of social research by two main ideas. First of all, it proposes to study society or a given community *in motion*, in a state of flux – a process that the research project itself has often precipitated. Secondly, action research takes the epistemological view about the nature and meaning of social scientific know-ledge that the ultimate purpose of knowledge and research lies in its ability to *change* social reality.

The view that social reality only exists in motion implies that unlike the traditional position, action research does not believe that the presence and the involvement of researchers, their interviews and observations, are a potential source of bias, a problem that must be resolved by spending a sufficient amount of time with the people who are being studied. By contrast, action research takes its point of departure from the notion that any research project always creates and inspires some move-ment in its object of study. Indeed the explicit purpose of action research is to create or accelerate movement so that its object of study is the *dynamics* of the group concerned or life in society. Society is not perceived as a static structure, nor is culture seen as a collectively shared *image* of the world, but it is held that 'society' and 'culture' only exist in movement, as laws of motion.

An outstanding example is the sociology of Alain Touraine (1981). According to Touraine, social life is a struggle over *historicity*, the direction of social and cultural development, and that struggle is waged between social movements that are formed on a class basis. Social movements, for Touraine, have a significance in themselves because it is through these move-ments that society is reproduced, that it is capable of self-corrective action. Movements retain this ability up to the point that they are institutionalized, when they become integrated into the state apparatus – which he says is what has happened to the trade union movement.

Touraine and his colleagues have indeed focused in their work on different kinds of social movements, including the labour movement, the student movement and the anti-nuclear movement. Through their 'sociological intervention', the re-searchers involved commit themselves to raising the standards of the movement's operation, to making them work more effectively; this is considered the right and proper task of research. Researchers will join these movements and within them try to inspire critical debate about the movement's goals and means, for instance by arranging public debates between the movement and its opponents. They will push the group beyond the purely ideological experience of membership towards critical self-reflection. The researchers will then use the material they accumulate in this process to write a detailed, analytical report on the intervention process.

The action research approach has been applied to many disciplines and fields of research, but not only purely academic researchers have found it a useful tool and working method. In fact, action researchers often emphasize that their approach differs from 'academic research'. For instance, it has been used in Third World countries as an integral part of development projects (Rigby 1977; Swantz and Bryceson 1976). It has also been applied by people researching and working in health and social care settings who have found it valuable in helping practitioners, managers and researchers to make sense of problems in service delivery and in promoting initiatives for change and improvement (Hart and Bond 1995). Furthermore, educational research has adopted it as one possible approach. McNiff (1994, 9) justifies its use by emphasizing that by consciously engaging in their own educational development, teachers gain both professionally and personally, and that it is the personal commitment that counts in the process of human inquiry.

As such the methodic premise of action research – that social phenomena should be approached as dynamic processes and that the subjects should be treated as equals with the researcher – are of course nothing new. Both these themes were raised earlier in our discussion of ethnographic research and especially so-called 'New Ethnography'. The same goes for the thesis that research should strive not to explain the world but to change it. Indeed this idea is central to Marx's *Theses on Feuerbach* (1845), the eleventh of which reads as follows: 'The philosophers have only *interpreted* the world in various ways; the point is to *change* it' (Marx 1976, 5). The use of scientific knowledge for purposes of social development has also been regarded as a key object in research aiming at 'human engineering' (Mills 1977, 127).

The difference between human engineering and action research is that in the latter case, the researcher sides with the oppressed and the underprivileged, trying to promote the changes that these people want to see, whereas human engineering is concerned to produce information that meets the needs of those in power. In this sense action research has a more sympathetic ring to it, but obviously it is necessary to have a more solid, theoretically grounded description of the research-er's role and position than this. On this account alone action research could justifiably set out to study neo-Nazis, help them better to explicate their interests and find the best way in which to attain those goals. After all neo-Nazis are a marginal group in society who are hunted and discriminated against.

It is clear, then, that it would be wrong automatically to suggest that action research is a more humane or a more ethical approach than the positivist approach which objectifies its subjects of study. The rational hard core of action research lies elsewhere: its conscious point of departure is the position that research is in itself a form of social action. The role of social research as a social institution, for its part, depends on the kind of subjects that are addressed and on how the research is reported. Action research does not just repeat this old wisdom, but it draws more radical conclusions. In the process of action research and in reporting on action research, special considera-tion is given to the impacts of research on the object of study and on society at large. An academic publication full of jargon, for instance, is unlikely to have very much impact beyond a small circle of intellectuals and civil servants who can decipher a text that for most people is gobbledegook. In other words, the language of research reports and the channels of publication are also part of the social scientists' politics, regardless of whether they are aware of this.

The specific concern of action research is thus with the impacts of research in society: both the immediate impacts it has in the object of study and its indirect impacts on public debate about the subject. However, it would be wrong to suggest that impact is the ultimate criterion of truth for action research, a principle followed in the spirit of pragmatism or some sort of Social Darwinism. In its quest for truth, action research does not differ in any way from other research orienta-tions because it has no distinctive theory of knowledge.

From this point of view the criticism that has been levelled against Touraine's method of sociological intervention for its strong researcher ethos, even its prophetism, is somewhat wide of the mark. The fact that the researchers, in Touraine's method, choose to focus on a collectivity that they believe represents a broader social movement does not mean that they should or could commit themselves to this sort of view. The researchers have no intention of elevating themselves to the supernatural status of an infallible prophet just because they happen to represent the scientific institution, they are simply doing their level best to uncover the truth. By reporting on the results of their study, the researchers are simply taking part in the public debate on society and its development. What sort of judgement is given of the researchers' capacities as prophets will depend on the reception of their ideas and on the programmes and actions their work inspires in society.

Generally accepted truths as a sociological problem

The production of French philosopher and sociologist Michel Foucault provides a different example of a research approach which takes into account the role of researcher and science as factors that are part of the phenomenon studied and that may therefore influence and change that phenomenon. One of Foucault's main interests was indeed with the sociology of knowledge, with the ways in which knowledge and the exercise of power in society are interwoven, but in his work he also came to formulate an important methodological principle; a vantage-point from which to approach concrete phenomena in research. That is, his studies of the history of Western civilization also look at the conceptions and the discourses that have informed earlier analyses of the phenomenon in question, both in academic research and in the general con-sciousness.

A brilliant example is provided by Foucault's history of sexuality. At the beginning of the first part of the trilogy Foucault (1978) reminds his readers about the story that 'Western' culture, leaning on an accumulating body of research evidence, tells itself about the history of sexuality. This is how Foucault says the story is told: For a long time we supported a Victorian regime, and we continue to be dominated by it even today. In the early seventeenth century a certain frankness was still common. Sexual practices had little need of secrecy; people still spoke openly, and things were done without too much concealment. There then followed an age of secrecy and repression, which was at its worst among the Victorian bourgeoisie. Sex moved into the home. The family was the only place where sex, for the serious function of reproduction, was accepted. Sex was silenced, hidden away. It did not occur anywhere in public, it had no right to. Everyone knew that children had no sex, which was why they were forbidden to talk about it. The moral climate became somewhat more relaxed from the late nineteenth century onwards. Perhaps some progress was made by Freud, although only in private, on the couch. This is why it is still necessary to have liberation and open debate on sexuality.

Foucault does not chronicle this generally accepted history only or primarily because he wants to prove it was wrong, or because he wants to turn our views upside-down. After all in the latter case nothing of any real consequence would change, only the signs. Rather, what he wants to do is address the specific question of why the Western view of the history of sexuality is organized by this 'repression hypothesis'. He wants to find out why modern society talks so much about its own silence, why it takes great pains to relate in detail things that it does not say. He does not ask, 'Why are we repressed?', but rather, 'Why do we say, with so much passion and so much resentment against our most resent past, against our present, and against ourselves, that we are repressed?'

It is true that Foucault does want to rewrite some parts of the history of sexuality, to demonstrate that many earlier views were wrong, that many turning-points in the history of sexuality have been misunderstood. For instance, he shows that during the era of Victorian 'silence' sexuality in its various forms became a more and more important part of all facets of life, that this era created an entire science, '*scientia sexualis*'. But this rewriting of history is not the crux of the matter. The key lies in Foucault's attempts to find a sociological explanation for the prevailing understanding of history and present-day reality. However, his research is not just high-brow sociology of knowledge; he also looks at the features of our sexual behaviour, our constant guilty conscience for failing to break loose from our inhibitions and to talk enough about sex. In other words, an important lesson is that our shared view of something and its history tends to influence our behaviour, and make its motivation more readily understandable. Scientific research is no exception in this regard, although this tends to be overlooked by researchers. The researcher is often blind to theorizing and to scientific debate, to the studies of other 'experts', which as far as the researcher is concerned fall outside his or her object of study. Other studies are easily treated as texts making impartial observations about the object of study. Typically, the researcher will only use other studies as points of comparison and as antitheses for his or her own observations and theses, without realizing that they do in fact constitute part of the researcher's object of study. This is not the case in Foucault's production, where earlier definitions and understandings of the phenomenon are recognized as an important part of the entity constituted by forms of power and knowledge and by patterns of behaviour.

Theoretical and methodological debate which recognizes the role of the researcher and research in society provides many useful clues or at least presents many challenging questions to researchers. First of all, researchers should always analyse their own personal and institutional status in conducting research so that they are aware at least of what sort of forces of change they may promote or prevent with their research results. The conclusions drawn from this sort of analysis should influence the way in which researchers approach their objects of study and how they place their words and which audiences they decide to address. Secondly, there are also methodological conclusions to be drawn from the involvement of science and research in social action in terms of how earlier research should be looked upon. It is important to realize that studies on a given phenomenon are in themselves part of that phenomenon. Social phenomena are never just 'behaviour' or 'structures' on which outside observers make observations and collect 'data'. Behaviour is always influenced by prevailing views on things, which also help to explain people's behaviour. What is more, distinctions between 'behaviour' and 'structures' or between 'structures' and 'consciousness' are in themselves historical and cultural rather than naturally existing differences.

Although these kinds of concepts and conceptual distinctions are used as research instruments outside the object of study, it is important to bear in mind that they, too, are part of the world-view whose restrictions and restrictiveness social research is out to break.

CHAPTER 7

STUDYING THE STRUCTURE OF SOCIAL REALITY

As was discussed earlier, all concepts appearing in the vocabulary of a given language are historical and cultural constructs; this has been the focal point of interest for the discipline known as semiotics or semiology. And it is not only concepts in language that consist of signs and symbols, the same applies to all our observations. As Charles S. Peirce pointed out in his pioneering researches, it is only by reading signs on the basis of what we have learned that we can 'see' what we think we are seeing.

Although often based on unconscious preconceptions about reality, the process of observation is essentially one of logical inference. This brings us to one side of semiotics, i.e. the study of the general principles of reading signs or drawing conclusions (which was discussed earlier in Chapter 3 where we looked at Holmes' method). Its roots can be traced back to medicine and pathology; this is how doctors have always made their diagnoses, by interpreting different kinds of symptoms. It is never the illness itself that presents itself to the doctor. Small wonder then that both Conan Doyle and Peirce were educated as medical doctors.

However, to revert to the question of concepts in language, the main difficulty lies not so much in how to understand them, but in how to persuade oneself not to believe that concepts refer to something fixed and permanent, to a reality that is independent of language and people. Empiricist research often falls into this trap as it sets out to tackle a given practical problem in society, such as racial or class differences in intelligence. Although the research design may be perfectly logical, using standardized control variables and control groups, the researcher is often tempted to take the concepts themselves (in this case 'race', 'intelligence' and 'class') more or less as given. In other words, the research design fails to recognize that 'race' cannot be detached from the related ethnic identity or from the social status of this ethnic group; that 'intelligence' is reducible to the items included in the IQ test and is therefore dependent on background and education; and that 'class' is also an historical category, its contents varying over time. This is the other side of semiotics: the study of the structure of signs and sign systems refers to the analysis of concepts into their constituent elements and to the search for their cultural and historical origins. In more general terms, this line of work aims to slot into their respective historical, social and cultural contexts such categories that people use in classifying and organizing social reality and in making sense of different social institutions. It involves a number of different research traditions: phenomenology, symbolic interactionism, ethnomethodology and social constructionism, all of which share a common interest in the role that language and other sign systems play in the construction of social reality. For simplicity, I will refer to all these lines of study by the single umbrella term of structuralism.

The research interest in the structure of the sign systems used in language and in society began to grow at around the same time as the general public began to read detective stories, i.e. in the early part of the twentieth century. The social circumstances which inspired this interest were no doubt very similar: with all the ongoing upheavals in society, many of the categories that had become established in industrial society were now proving more or less fragile and variable in content. Inevitably, Einstein's theory of relativity and the continuing growth and expansion of the urban milieu also affected people's views on nature. According to Henri Lefebvre (1971), it is possible to date these changes quite accurately. Some 100 years ago, Lefebvre says, the world and society still appeared to the Europeans as clear and coherent systems. Therefore each concept still had a distinct referent in reality. People still had a clear, shared view on the meaning of ethics, aesthetics, honour, honesty and self-respect. Around 1905–1910, with the changes that were taking place in science, technology and society at large, the referents of these taken-for-granted concepts began to break down.

Yet it was still only a fairly small group of intellectuals who were affected by these changes in ways of thinking. Their impacts, Lefebvre says, were restricted to elitist painting and music. This period around the turn of the century saw the development of abstract art and atonal music, for instance.

On a larger scale the structuralist or *linguistic turn* has had a more profound impact on the social sciences only since the mid-1950s. The main force behind this turn was the French anthropologist Claude Lévi-Strauss, whose *Structural Anthropology* was published in French in 1958 and in English in 1963. In the 1960s the work generated an entire structuralist movement, whose influence extended to numerous anthropological disciplines and schools. By the end of the 1960s, structuralism came under sharp attack from a new, post-structuralist school, but it weathered the storm and has in fact remained one of the most important isms of social theory up to the present day. Its basic tenets have continued to enjoy widespread appeal regardless of all the crises that have swept across Western society.

Language as a closed system

Like many innovations created in response to a social demand, semiotics (understood in its broadest sense) has many fathers and intellectual antecedents. These include Charles S. Peirce (1839–1914) as well as George Herbert Mead (1863–1931), who from the year 1900 onwards began work on a theory of human activity and thinking that was later to become known as symbolic interactionism. Mead argued that objects in social reality exist through adaptation to or interpretation of the meaning of a given gesture or communication between individuals (Mead 1962 [1934]).

However, the theorist who has most influenced our views on the relationship between linguistic and other signs and reality is Swiss linguist Ferdinand de Saussure (1857–1913). Unlike Peirce, whose theories were based on the distinction between object, the sign representing the object and the interpretation offered of the object, and unlike Mead, who said that meaning came from the interpretation given to a gesture in social interaction, in his theory of the nature of language and other sign systems Saussure concentrates exclusively on signs. His argument was that the tangible object, known as the referent, serves only to confuse things, and prevents us from realizing the essence of sign. In his view language must be examined as a closed system which consists exclusively of signs and their mutual relationships.

The sign, then, consists of two analytically distinct elements, *signifier* and *signified*. Signifier refers to the sound-image that makes up the word (such as 'tree'), while signified refers to the concept tree, the meaning of the said sound-image. When we hear the word 'tree', we realize that it means tree.

Saussure points out that the relationship between signifier and signified, between the meaning of the sound-image and the concept associated with that meaning, is wholly arbitrary and artificial: it is impossible to infer from the word's acoustic image what it means. Although some words that describe sounds are onomatopoeic, i.e. they are formed by copying that sound, Saussure points out that these words are different in different languages and do not provide a sufficiently solid and broad basis for theory-building. The meaning of each word must quite simply be learned.

The meaning of an individual term will depend on the meaning of other terms. The most important aspect about language as a closed system is the ability of an individual term to stand apart from all other terms, which determines what each concept means. The same applies to the level of individual phonemes, and to written language as well. Consider a handwritten essay that a teacher is marking. It will be no major problem for the teacher if the letter 'r', for instance, is not written exactly according to the book so long as it is clearly distinguishable from the letter 'v'. If the student has a clear and consistent system of distinctions, the teacher will have little difficulty reading the text as soon as a few familiar words have helped to 'break the code'. In other words, language is a *system of differences*, a series of differences of sound combined with a series of differences of ideas (Saussure 1966, 120 [1915]).

The same principle of arbitrariness applies to the scope of an individual concept. The concept that is expressed in a word,

Saussure says, is not a name for an object in the reality located outside language. The scope covered by the concept is not given in reality, but again language relies on conventions; it is a closed system in which the scope of a concept is determined by its relationship to other concepts. Saussure (ibid., 115–116) refers here to the difference between the French word 'mouton' and the English 'mutton': the French word refers both to the living animal and to its meat; mutton refers only to the latter. In Saussure's terms, the word 'mutton' has a different *value* than the word 'mouton'; English additionally needs the word 'sheep' to cover the same scope, the same value as the French word 'mouton'.

These theses seem to conflict with the commonsensical notion that language names the objective reality we perceive, and that language provides a tool with which we can describe that reality. We are prepared to accept that the same object (say a tree) can mean different things to different people, as Blumer (1986, 11) observes in introducing the basic tenets of symbolic interactionism: 'a tree will be a different object to a botanist, a lumberman, a poet, and a home gardener'. Yet we will still insist that a tree is a tree. The problem with this way of thinking, Saussure points out, is that tree is a *concept* which classifies reality, not the name of a specific object in nature. In the Finnish language, for instance, the word 'puu' refers to both growing trees and felled timber; the scope or 'value' (as Saussure has it) of the English-language concept of tree is thus smaller than that of the Finnish concept. The point must also be made that the distinction between a 'tree' and a 'bush', for example, depends on how a (linguistic) community defines a 'tree' in relation to other plants and living creatures. In other words, this is not simply a matter of semantics, but a much more far-reaching issue: reality presents itself as distinct objects and beings that are distinguished from one another on the basis of a collective system of distinctions. In a rainbow, for instance, there are no dividing lines at the places that we consider to mark the boundaries between different colours; the spectrum is simply a continuum in which the wavelength of the light increases across the arch of colours. The way in which we divide this continuum into colours with different names is based on a system of distinctions that is specific to our culture, not to nature. Indeed, different cultures divide the rainbow in different ways into different colours (Eco 1976). The same view is contained in the Sapir–Whorf hypothesis (named after American linguists Edward Sapir and Benjamin Whorf), which says that the structure of a language tends to condition the ways in which a speaker of that language organizes nature, slots it into different categories and interprets it (Whorf 1956, 213).

From all that has been said above it does not follow, however, that our observations are arbitrary, or that the semiotic framework rejects the notion of a reality that is independent of consciousness. The concern here is strictly with the *nature* of the reality we observe: a reality that is socially determined through and through. The way in which we perceive reality, divide it up into distinct categories, is a *systemic entity*, but that entity is not dictated by nature but rather by cultural tradition and life-practices. It cannot be at sharp variance with the laws of nature and other factors that are external to it, because otherwise it would be impossible to cope with practical situations. It is for this reason that changes in living conditions, whether resulting from changes in technology or natural conditions, also influence the way we perceive reality. New frames of interpretation need to be developed in place of the old ones that no longer work. However, the changes are never perfect because the new living conditions and the challenges they pose will be examined within the framework of the old models.

Physical and social reality

Saussure's theory of general linguistics provides a useful account of the nature of the system that we use in observing the world and of how that system works. Although confined to the analysis of the nature of language, the theory does provide a framework for studying the different classification systems that are used in observing the world. For Saussure, language is a special case, one part of the totality of sign systems which organize social interaction. It is clear that language has its own distinctive features and that the individual's ability to perceive the world is not restricted to linguistic concepts, to what is possible within the confines of those concepts; if that were the case, then obviously the ways of perceiving the world that are typical of each culture could not change with changing circumstances. Nonetheless language does have a major influence on our thinking, our mutual understanding, our action, and the way our action is interpreted.

However, the structuralist view on the relationship between language and reality should not be seen simply as a theory concerning the psychology of perception. This implies a very narrow focus on the relationship between concepts in language and material nature, with concepts examined simply as words that describe, classify and name the outside reality. Yet social reality consists for the main part of concepts and conceptual distinctions that have no referent in the reality that is independent of language and its concepts. Take the concept of democracy. Countless debates and conflicts and wars have been waged over the definition of democracy, both for and against the kind of democracy that the term is generally thought to mean. Although the parties to these debates and conflicts may have appealed to nature, arguing that theirs is the 'natural' way to understand democracy, this hardly gives reason to assume that these kinds of concepts originate from nature. Most of the concepts which organize social reality have no referent in the material nature, but that does not mean to say that the concepts concerned are imaginary or irrelevant. On the contrary, social reality is constructed out of these concepts and can only be understood through them.

Structuralism's main contribution to sociological research has indeed been in the form of conceptual tools for an analysis of the way in which social reality is constructed. Although the structuralist turn at the beginning of the twentieth century was related in part to the breakthroughs in the natural sciences, most notably the introduction of the theory of relativity and quantum theory, semiotics (as Saussure predicted) has achieved its most significant results in studying the 'life of signs in society'.

One of Ferdinand de Saussure's contemporaries who was greatly influenced by the structuralist revolution was Émile Durkheim, better known for the pioneering work he did in quantitative social research. In *The Elementary Forms of the Religious Life* Durkheim (1954 [1912]) explores the social origins of concepts in a manner very reminiscent of Saussure's theories.

The indigenous tribes that Durkheim studied were always divided into clans: groups whose members said they were related to each other. This kinship is based on the belief that the clan is descended from its totem: an animal, plant or sometimes a natural object. Each clan has its own sacred totem, a god-like creature. Furthermore, the tribe that is divided into clans is usually divided into two phratries, which consist of a group of clans united to each other by particular bonds of phratry.

Nature is divided into classes according to the same system that divided the tribe into phratries and clans. Each living or inanimate creature belongs to some clan. Not only animals, plants and humans, but also the stars in the sky and natural phenomena are classified according to the same principles. For the tribe, the universe is a major tribe with everything living and everything inanimate slotted into some department.

Totemism provides for the natives a complete world-view, a cosmological order with its own systematics and internal logic. For example, the Mount Gambier tribe was divided into the phratries of Kumite and Kroki. While winter, rain, thunder, lightning, clouds, hail, the stars and the moon belonged to the Kumite phratry, the Kroki phratry had the summer, sun, wind and autumn. In other words if the sun belongs to one phratry, the moon belongs to another one. The totemistic world-view is thus based on comparisons, distinctions and juxtapositions – an idea familiar from structuralism.

Durkheim says that the key thing about his study of totemism is the discovery that the notion of class as well as any systems of classification used by world cultures have a social origin. Although the decision to slot two creatures into the same category may be inspired by visible similarities, the idea of the category comes from human society and not from nature. The same principles are used to divide natural creatures and phenomena into clans and phratries as are applied to the tribe's social organization.

Durkheim's study also sheds interesting light on the special nature of social reality. One of the clans belonging to the Kumite phratry in the Mount Gambier tribe was the clan of the crow. The members of this clan believed they were descended from some mythical crow and accordingly that they were related to crows. An outsider might try to convince these people that it is impossible for a human being to be a descendant of a crow, but this natural science argumentation has no relevance in trying to understand the behaviour or 'nature' of the members of this clan. They *are* like crows, they behave like crows because they themselves and the members of other clans regard them as members of the crow clan and base their interpretations of their behaviour on that assumption. The crow in question is not the bird that appears in birdwatchers' handbooks; this crow refers to the tribe which in addition to crows and the human members of the clan includes rain, thunder, lightning, clouds, hail and winter. The crow clan is characterized by what the natives regard as features that all these creatures share in common. This could be compared to the arguments we have in modern society about what is characteristically feminine or masculine. The arguments that a woman is 'feminine' or that the member of the crow clan is 'crow-like' cannot be denounced as irrelevant simply on grounds that they have no validity from a natural science point of view. If people rely in their everyday life on these sorts of concepts, they are concrete elements of social reality.

The concepts we use in examining social reality and in interpreting social action are not based on the 'real' nature of physical reality, but on the systemic entity of distinctions and comparisons within which individual concepts make sense. Talk about 'femininity' is meaningful only in so far as it is possible to identify a counterpart: things or behaviours that are *not* regarded as feminine. These construct 'masculinity'. On the other hand, it has to be possible to qualify such talk and give examples of feminine behaviour, comparable things that reflect femininity, to identify what is common in these examples, i.e. 'femininity'. The concepts are thus based on distinctions and comparisons.

The structure of modern everyday life: a short history

Modern society can also be examined as a totemistic system in which the classification systems used in examining the world have their equivalent in the social organization and institutional order of society. The best examples are to be found within the structuration of everyday life since industrialism. This has been studied in a structuralist spirit especially in research on the social history of the working classes.

The wage labourer's everyday life is organized into three domains: work, leisure and family life. These domains can also be clearly identified in the physical structures of any modern city. Even in the oldest countries of the Industrial Revolution the history of these distinct spheres goes back no more than some 100 years, yet this social organization of everyday life has shaped modern people and their collective imagination in some very crucial ways.

In a study of the industrial town of Worcester on the east coast of America, Roy Rosenzweig (1983) describes the development from the 1870s onwards of an area dedicated to leisure pursuits, distinct from both work and family life. In the late nineteenth century it was still considered natural for people to socialize and to attend to any common business they had in the factory during working hours. It was quite common for people to drink rum at work, and they could easily spare the time given the leisurely pace of their 12-hour days. The pace of work was stepped up, however, with the introduction (in response to growing worker demands) of shorter hours. Drinking in the workplace was also forbidden, as were all kinds of socializing. This created a demand for working-class saloons outside the factory gates. In a sense, a slice of the working day was set aside for social relations and relaxation. At the same time the kitchen barrooms that women operated in private homes were outlawed; these had been particularly popular among the Irish. Running saloons became a purely commercial business, at the same time as leisure and its various domains became a prerogative for males.

The history of the British working class follows the same pattern. It also provides interesting insights into the way in which the history of gender relations is interwoven with industrialism. From the late eighteenth century onwards the industrial population, recruited from the ranks of the rural landless, had become used to the whole family, including all the children, working together all day long. This was in fact their only option because the wages in industry were not enough for the head of the family to support them all. On the other hand, there was no public system of children's day care, so in a sense the use of child labour helped to resolve any day care problems as well. The growth of the weaving industry had also greatly reduced women's chances of making a living in home industry. When industrial wages eventually began to rise and the use of child labour was forbidden, women stayed at home as soon as the family could afford this. This was not a matter of restoring the old patriarchal order as soon as this became financially possible. Rather, the use of female labour during the early stages of industrialization had left women with the worst possible deal both in the home and in the factory: as they were recruited to work in factories women had lost the greater personal freedom they had enjoyed in home industry, but at the same time they were still left with their second role as mother and housewife (Thompson 1963). The new order of everyday life, with the woman looking after the home and the children and the husband going out to earn a living for the family, helped to establish a new division of spheres and the related collective imagination: the factory and leisure, the public domain, was a male sphere, and the privacy of the home was a female sphere. In the 1870s the distinction between these male and female domains was further underlined as the working-class living quarters in London, for instance, moved further away from the factory gates and separate suburbs were built. The contradictions of the new order of life were reflected in the songs of the music halls (Jones 1983).

The main lesson of social-historical research inspired by semiotics is that the structure of the life-order of a certain society cannot be taken to have one single root cause or starting-point. Social life is always already organized by a given structure, and the sudden changes occurring in living conditions will see a *transformation* of that structure rather than its replacement. The research evidence indicates that cultural classification systems are incredibly persistent, even when external conditions are completely changed.

Life-style and homological relations

Structuralism has also been a major influence in research on modern cultures, especially in the work of Pierre Bourdieu and the so-called Birmingham School of cultural studies. In their analyses of the internal structure of people's way of life, both these approaches rely to a great extent on the concept of *homology*.

Bourdieu has studied the cultural class structure of French society using material which describes the consumption patterns of French people and their tastes in art (Bourdieu 1984). According to Bourdieu, people's leisure interests and taste in art, for instance, are good indicators of social status and educational level. Bourdieu observes that music taste in particular is a highly accurate measure that clearly distinguishes individuals in different social status positions. The most interesting thing about Bourdieu's studies is the way in which he uses consumption surveys to explore the French class structure. Unlike the traditional survey researcher, Bourdieu is not applying a causal model to try to *explain* the way of life of individuals, suggesting, for instance, that these people with this educational level or income belong to this social class. In fact he reverses the whole setting: from Bourdieu's viewpoint artists are artists for the very reason that they like Andy Warhol and avant-garde festivals and know about the theories of the *Tel Quel* group (Bourdieu 1984, 128). Bourdieu detects from his material social groupings who differ from other groupings in terms of their taste and habits: they like the same kind of music, food, clothes and leisure activities. He studies these kinds of statistical relationships between the individual's way of life and tastes as evidence of the existence of a *habitus*, a certain way of thinking and acting that organizes the individual's everyday life, that is typical of each social class or stratum.

It is here, in his analyses of the nature of habitus, that Bourdieu employs the concept of *homology*. Habitus is based not only on distinctions but also on parallels: for example, Bourdieu says that windsurfing, Van Gogh and ceramics go together because they all reflect the same habitus that is characteristic of cultural workers. There is a *homological relationship* between them; they are different kinds of expressions of the same style. To reconstruct the habitus that is characteristic of different groups of people, Bourdieu uses qualitative materials and the empathetic imagination he possesses as a member of French culture to lay bare the world-view to which the various indicators of a certain group's way of life provide important clues.

In the 1970s the Birmingham School took a somewhat different approach in their studies, many of which were based on
ethnographic materials. Nonetheless the concept of homology is
an important methodological tool for the Birmingham School as
well, particularly in the work of Paul Willis.

The Birmingham School's studies were typically focused on
an individual cultural group, for instance a youth subculture
(e.g. Hall and Jefferson 1975; Hebdige 1979). The analysis
would be concerned with the meanings assumed within the
group by different objects and activities, and those meanings
would then be compared with each other. In this sense homological analysis is comparative research in that it aims to
uncover the internal logic of a view of life by studying its
manifestations. Leisure activities or characteristics of a life-style
that are important to the individual and to a cultural group not
only reflect style, but also influence their cultural identity:

> The essential base of a *homological* cultural relation is that an
> artefact or object has the ability to reflect, resonate and sum up
> crucial values, states, and attitudes for the social group involved
> within it. The artefact or object must consistently serve the group
> with the meanings, attitudes and certainties it wants, and it must
> support and return, and substantiate central life meanings. One
> can understand this partly as communication, but much more
> profoundly it should be understood as a process of cultural resona-
> tion, and concretization of identity. (Willis 1974, 11)

A classical example is Willis's analysis of a motorbike group in
his *Profane Culture* (1978). All the members of the group are
working-class lads, and Willis argues that their cultural forms
continue the traditions of working-class culture. Looking at the
group from the outside, this seems a strange argument: their
parents would never even think of driving around on bikes or
listening to 1950s rock'n'roll. Indeed the link to the parent
culture is to be found at the symbolic level. For the group
members, Willis says, the bike represents a relationship to
nature, the arduous struggle to gain control over nature that on
the factory shopfloor goes on in the form of manual work. This
helps to explain why the lads drive around without crash
helmets and why they have fitted their bikes with chopper-style
handlebars so that they sit in an upright position. Although this

slows them down, speed is not essential; the key thing is to feel the air-flow which threatens to throw them off the bike. It is for the same reason that they opt not to wear crash helmets.

It is of course an analytical and methodic solution to study life-style on the basis of the concept of homology; homologies do not float about in the reality 'out there', waiting to be identified and described. However, this kind of cultural research is not about deducing reality from a theory and forcing it into a set pattern. The homologies are not in this case identified and determined by theory, nor does the theory determine what kind of entity these homologies constitute.

The methodic principle applied in the search for homologies can be compared to the semiotic view of language. Say that we have a group of punk rockers explaining what punk means to them. Since they are talking about an idea that they all share in common, about a way of life, an internal link has to exist between the various facets or elements of this life-style. Style is an organized assembly of its different manifestations, which can be described in different 'languages': in music, in dress, in behaviour. One of these manifestations may shed light on things from just one particular point of view, but when the group explains how that relates to the broader picture, the whole idea finds expression even within the single individual element. Therefore matters reflecting the same style appear as homological to one another. However, style, in the sense of this kind of all-pervasive idea, is not reduced to any single element reflecting or defining it, nor to any external cause or factor. The same applies to terms in language. The relationship of individual elements of a style to the whole reminds us of how the sign is defined in structural linguistics and semiotics: this relationship is one where each element refers to the rest without this relationship being predetermined by the nature of any one of them (Laclau 1983, 40).

The choice to use the concept of homology to explain the leisure interests or the attitudes of an individual or a cultural group does not mean that we are assuming the individual's life-style constitutes a harmonious whole. Leisure interests and attitudes are not only invariable elements within a constant meaning structure, but they have their own specific function. That is, the individual and the group have to take most of their living conditions as given. The individual is born as a man or a woman, it is easiest for practical reasons for the individual to do a certain job, and so on. These kinds of external conditions and social determinants of life have a major impact on the shape of the individual's everyday life and very much restrict his or her opportunities to organize it differently. Within the confines of those conditions and determinants, individuals will try to find attitudes and leisure interests through which they can study their life, shape it to better suit their interests and to find a meaning and order to their existence. Spontaneous, independent activity, whether in the form of belonging to a youth culture or going to the theatre, serves the function of allowing the individual or the group to test, at a symbolic level, the applicability of different attitudes and styles to their own situation. Leisure activities rarely help to improve the individual's position at work, but they may illustrate and reinforce an attitude which helps to preserve the individual's self-respect.

Although homology is a relatively recent term that was introduced within structuralism, the same basic idea of explanation can be traced back much further. One of the studies in which it appears is William Foote Whyte's *Street Corner Society* (1981 [1943]). Following the work of the Chicago School, the study focuses on a youth gang in the Italian quarter of an American city. Each gang, Whyte says, has a strict social hierarchy consisting of the gang leader, his 'lieutenants' and other, rank-and-file members within a certain hierarchic order. The hierarchy is extremely rigid and it would not be permissible for a gang member to borrow money, for instance, from someone lower down in the hierarchy: you cannot be dependent on a lower-ranking group member for very long. There are also strict limits and procedural rules for making suggestions on how the gang spends its time. Direct submissions to the leader may come only from lieutenants; if someone else in the hierarchy has an idea, that will have to go through official channels to the lieutenants, who will then take the message to the leader. Whyte compares this hierarchy to the Catholic world-view that is represented by Italians as well as to the cosmological order, which reflects the worldly social organization in a corresponding manner. Italians have the same hierarchic approach in religion. Whenever they have a problem they do not (unlike

Protestants) turn directly to God but go to their patron saint, who will speak to God on their behalf.

The ontology of structure

The structuralist approach is one of the tools available to social scientists who want to find something that all subjects share in common or (if the research material consists of popular customs or historical events) something that could be described as the highest common denominator of the material. The approach can be applied to ethnographic research, as the Birmingham School has shown, but it is also applicable to the analysis of many other kinds of materials. It is also well suited to the comprehensive analysis of modern society with its disparate groups of people with very different world-views and attitudes to life. That is, the focal concern in structuralist research is with language and other sign systems used in human communication as well as with the distinction and classification systems that organize social action. If it can be shown that a systematic entity, a cultural unconscious, lies behind individual differences in attitudes and behaviour, helping to explain and make these differences understandable in a broader context, then we can shift our attention from individual differences and address instead the question of what makes even the random group of separate individuals a community.

Structuralism starts out from the presumption that each culture has its own distinctive structure of the collective unconscious, which is primary in relation to people and their opinions and ways of thinking. In the words of the father of modern structuralism, Claude Lévi-Strauss, 'We don't attempt to demonstrate how men [and women] think through myths, but how myths think themselves through men' (cited in Shalvey 1979, 35). This actually involves two closely related presumptions. There is huge variation in the extent to which different schools that have been influenced by structuralism stress the aspect of structure in relation to subjects, those who are making observations of the world and changing the world on the basis of their interpretations. On the other hand, swearing by structure raises the question of its ontological status. In what sense does this kind of structure of collective consciousness exist?

This latter question has occupied a central place especially in the French debate on social philosophy. The views raised in this debate are often described as post-structuralism. According to the most outstanding figure of post-structuralism, Jacques Derrida, Lévi-Strauss does not properly follow up the conclusions that can be drawn from his thesis that the individual's thinking is secondary to the structures of language and collective unconsciousness. In denying self-sufficient logic and order at the individual level, he transfers it to the level of the collective unconscious. The structures of culture and cultural products appear to Lévi-Strauss as unchangeable. Derrida says that Lévi-Strauss's thinking, in this respect, represents a 'metaphysics of presence': it assumes by default that the structures of the collective consciousness are real, fixed and timeless. Derrida (1976), on the other hand, looks upon language as an assembly of rival and mutually conflicting discourses and textual levels; the text is never closed as far as its meanings are concerned.

Derrida's method of deconstructionism is in many ways an extension to the structuralism that started with Saussure. He, too, is concerned with texts and the systems of distinction they contain, albeit at a different level. Derrida is not interested in studying everyday reality; instead, his analysis of the contradictions hidden in the texts of social theorists amounts to a 'critique of critique'. The difference with more 'orthodox' structuralist social research is that the *structures* of consciousness and texts are given only a methodic role rather than using them to build an ontological theory of the essence of reality.

All in all the post-structuralist tradition, including the work of Derrida and Michel Foucault and many others, clearly illustrates the presumption contained within the structuralist approach, i.e. the view that meaning is based on systems of difference. Post-structuralism tests the limits imposed by this presumption by criticizing all easy solutions. This is probably its major contribution: it reminds us that whenever reality is simplified or reduced to its 'essence', something is pushed aside, swept under the carpet. It reminds us that at the end of the day, the most important thing of all for critical social research is what does not fit into the assumed order: that which appears as irrelevant from the point of view of the prevailing theory, which remains hidden or invisible. Contradictions and antinomies are the seeds of new ideas. However, they need fertile soil in which to grow. Post-structuralism, for instance, will go nowhere without the structuralist carpet of meanings, for it builds its theories out of crumbs that have been swept under that carpet.

CHAPTER 8

FROM THE STUDY OF CULTURAL PRODUCTS TO NARRATIVE ANALYSIS

In recent years cultural studies of modern societies have shown a growing interest in different kinds of cultural products such as films, life stories, advertisements and jokes. At the same time, the methodological developments in the study of cultural products have clearly exposed the problems involved in a structuralist framework. There has been a movement away from textual analysis towards studies of reading and interpretation, and to analysis of the reception and production of stories.

The study of cultural products can be seen as one way of applying the basic idea of a qualitative approach to modern, individualized society: since it is hard to come to grips with features that distinct individuals share in common by means of interviews or by case studies of disparate small communities, a useful alternative is provided by the study of the stories that the individuals tell each other. Instead of a whole sample of interviewees, the object of study may consist of one single story, a genre of stories, or a certain theme appearing in different stories.

This kind of material is readily available. It is also better suited to a 'thicker' description and interpretation than a superficial survey analysis of data collected in structured interviews. Having said that, it must be stressed that cultural documents are of a particular nature. Unlike statistical survey data, films, commercials or jokes cannot be regarded as realistic or representative pictures of an empirical reality. Their relation to reality is more complex – and, as far as the purposes of cultural studies are concerned, more interesting. The aim of cultural studies is to appraise the cultural structures in terms of which people conceive the world and which constitute the particular, historical conditions under which even hard economic facts come true. Cultural models and stereotypes manifest themselves in crystallized form in films, commercials, jokes and autobiographies.

In the study of stories, cultural models or schemes can be seen at the level of the macrostructures of language. This means that the focal concern is not with the rules followed in formulating individual sentences, but with the structural features or the 'grammar of stories' appearing in larger textual wholes.

Most of the work so far has concentrated on the narrative structure of stories. The concept of narrative structure refers to two different traditions or main trends of structuralism, described by Maranda and Köngäs Maranda (1971), using concepts adopted from linguistics, as the paradigmatic and the syntagmatic trends.

The paradigmatic trend

Paradigmatic analysis is concerned not with the logic of the story or with how it unfolds chronologically, but with the relations of meaning between separate terms or parts of the story. Claude Lévi-Strauss had a pioneering role in developing this school of thought with his analyses of the structure of myths. Paraphrasing the well-known structuralist linguist Roman Jakobson, Lévi-Strauss argued that the meaning of myths can be traced back to a limited number of binary oppositions, the constituent units of all signification. According to Lévi-Strauss's theory, the plot of a story is merely a surface; the essential content of a myth can be grasped only by breaking down the story into separate sentences and by rearranging them in an appropriate manner. Lévi-Strauss groups together all sentences signifying a similar relation into a limited number of bundles. For example, in his programmatic article on the structural study of myth (Lévi-Strauss 1968, 206–231) he distinguishes in the Oedipus myth a mytheme by the name 'underrating of blood relations', signified in the story by the following sentences: 'The Spartoi kill one another', 'Oedipus kills his father, Laius', and 'Eteocles kills his brother, Polynices'. These bundles of relations or mythemes, Lévi-Strauss says, are related to one another by forming binary oppositions among themselves, and together they comprise the meaning structure of the myth.

One of the few Finnish empirical applications of the paradigmatic trend in the field of cultural studies, 'Drinking on the Screen: An Analysis of a Mythical Male Fantasy in Finnish Films', by Falk and Sulkunen (1983), follows Lévi-Strauss's method quite literally. The study is an excellent demonstration of the way in which mythical deep structures are linked with the social and historical background.

The research material consisted of scenes of drunkenness in Finnish films. The researchers took detailed notes of the events, and then broke their notes down into mythemes or units composed of incidents that were as limited as possible in their scope. These units, some of which consisted simply of separate replies, were classified and reorganized, finally yielding a sort of triangle of the mythical structure of drunkenness. The points of the triangle, signifying different aspects of the myth, were named as incompatibility between alcohol and women; empty solidarity among the drinking men; and cosmic solitude of the man who is drunk.

Incompatibility between alcohol and women was manifested in the material in three ways. Firstly, alcohol served for men as a substitute for women: for instance, a rejected man may start to drink and get drunk. Secondly, women are excluded by alcohol, i.e. they are generally excluded from the drinking circle, or once they are included, they are treated as whores. Thirdly, women have an external role in relation to male drunkenness. That is, women are present only as fictitious or anonymous objects of pleasure, or as a source of external control or servant, as in the role of waitress.

The theme of *empty solidarity among the drinking men* was evident in the fact that the social position of a man would not affect his value or position in the drinking circle. However, the internal solidarity of the group only extends to drinking camaraderie, to secure the continuity of the drinking bout. Otherwise, the men in the group of drinkers are indifferent to one another's worries, and what look like confidences are in fact insignificant.

By the *cosmic solitude of the man who is drunk*, Falk and Sulkunen refer to the drinking scenes in which, in a variety of ways, men seem to reflect on the origin of man, his cosmic situation, and the contrast between life and death. The men often give expression to drunkenness as a symbol of death by pretending to fly, which is associated with the fear of falling down. The men's relation to nature is manifested as a contradiction between submission to the forces of nature, on the one hand, and control over nature, on the other.

Falk and Sulkunen illustrate the internal structure of the mythical triangle they have developed by transforming it 'back' into a form of a story, a sort of master narrative. A man who is drunk leaves social normality, represented by a woman, depends on the shelter provided by the group of drinkers, and ends up in a state of cosmic loneliness. This theme, which manifests itself in a host of cultural products (e.g. in the lyrics of songs), is, according to Falk and Sulkunen, a mythical expression of the disappearance of peasant culture and of the creation of a class of wage-earners. These developmental trends in Finnish society have brought about a crisis of patriarchy and thus contributed to the creation of these male fantasies manifested in the mythical structure of drunkenness, which then serves to prop up the masculine identity.

The syntagmatic trend

The other main branch of structuralist approaches to the study of narratives stems from the method originally developed for an analysis of folk tales by Russian folklorist Vladimir Propp in the late 1920s. Propp's concept of structure refers to the form by which the events of a story are logically and chronologically linked together to make up the plot. Unlike Lévi-Strauss, who is concerned not with the synchronic unfolding of the narrative but rather with the relations of meaning between different parts of a story, Propp studied tales as wholes, as series of consecutive events through which the state of affairs described at the beginning of the story transformed into something else.

Propp's method is particularly useful for the classification of plot structures.

Propp's great invention was to define the type of tale on the basis of the totality that is manifested by its plot. The plot structure is made up of constituent units or functions, which he defined as follows: 'Function is understood as an act of a character, defined from the point of view of its significance for the course of action' (Propp 1975, 21 [1928]). It follows from this definition that an identical act may represent different functions, depending on its function for the unfolding of the plot. If, for instance, Ivan marries the daughter of the Tsar, this is entirely different from the marriage of a father to a widow with two daughters. On the other hand, different objects may serve the same function, as is clear from Propp's (ibid., 19–20) example of manifestations of the same function:

1. A tsar gives an eagle to a hero. The eagle carries the hero away to another kingdom.
2. An old man gives Sucenko a horse. The horse carries Sucenko away to another kingdom.
3. A sorcerer gives Ivan a little boat. The boat takes Ivan to another kingdom.

Propp discovered in his studies of Russian fairy tales that functions serve as stable, constant elements of a tale, independent of how and by whom they are fulfilled. The number of functions appearing in a group of stories within the same narrative tradition – in this case Russian fairy tales – is quite limited when compared with the multi-faceted outlook of the tales. According to Propp's idea, tales may be said to represent the same type when their plot structure consists of the same functions appearing in the same chronological order. However, not all functions have to appear in one individual fairy tale. Rather, the morphology of a tale type is a sort of master tale, so that individual stories can be conceived of as variants of that tale.

In the case of the material that Propp studied – tales numbered 300 to 749 and named as fairy tales in A. Aarne's tale type index – it turned out that all of the 100 tales in the sample represented the same type. This tale type consisted of 31 consecutive functions, which Propp named according to their content. One can therefore get an idea of the content of these tales, in all their different variations, by reading the list of functions identified by Propp, the first three of which are as follows: (1) Absentation: one of the members of a family absents himself from home; (2) interdiction: an interdiction is addressed to the hero and (3) violation: the interdiction is violated. In other words, the plot starts to unfold when, for instance, the parents leave for work, or when the children go out to pick berries. In spite of an interdiction, such as 'Take care of your little brother, do not venture forth from the courtyard', a family member violates the order. As can be guessed, the family becomes liable to some misfortune, damage or harm caused by the villain who enters the tale.

Propp's method is quite easy to learn and can be used for the empirical analysis of many kinds of stories. However, the method includes no in-built interpretation as to the kind of society that has created a particular genre of stories. That is why those who have applied it have usually combined the syntagmatic method in one way or another with a paradigmatic analysis.

From morphology to mythology

Will Wright has combined syntagmatic and paradigmatic approaches in an elegant way in his study *Sixguns and Society* (1977), which looks at the relation between American society and Western films. Wright starts out with a morphological analysis of the films in his sample, and then interprets the results on the basis of Lévi-Straussian myth theory.

Wright found that there were four story types in the Westerns he studied: the classical plot, the vengeance variation, the transition theme and the professional plot. Wright names the functions of the classical plot as follows:

1. The hero enters a social group.
2. The hero is unknown to the society.
3. The hero is revealed to have an exceptional ability.
4. The society recognizes a difference between themselves and the hero; the hero is given a special status.

5. The society does not completely accept the hero.
6. There is a conflict of interests between the villains and the society.
7. The villains are stronger than the society; the society is weak.
8. There is a strong friendship or respect between the hero and a villain.
9. The villains threaten the society.
10. The hero avoids involvement in the conflict.
11. The villains endanger a friend of the hero.
12. The hero fights the villains.
13. The hero defeats the villains.
14. The society is safe.
15. The society accepts the hero.
16. The hero loses or gives up his special status.

Wright goes on to describe in a corresponding way the three other plot variants, and analyses the world-views that they represent on the basis of Lévi-Strauss's ideas. He shows that these historically consecutive plot variants represent different ways of dealing with the tension between individual and society. While in the classical plot the hero helps the society because it is weak, in the vengeance variation and in the transition theme the hero steps outside of society for the same reason: the weak society is unable to punish the villains and therefore the hero himself takes revenge for the injustices he has suffered. In the professional plot the hero is permanently outside of society, and the question of good and bad, right and wrong, has lost its meaning. Gunfighting is the hero's profession and a source of excitement.

Although the Westerns representing different plot variants have to some extent been produced contemporaneously, they generally follow each other historically. The classical plot Westerns were produced in 1930–1955, the vengeance variations in 1948–1961, the transition themes in 1950–1954 and the professional plot Westerns from 1959 onwards. This, Wright suggests, corresponds to the shift in American society from market capitalism to corporate capitalism.

Wright's theoretical and methodological solutions in this study, as well as the problems of his ambitious research, make this a particularly interesting example. Although his efforts to link the plot variants to the structural changes in American society remain quite loose and sketchy, it is still a challenging and inspiring piece of work. The result of his structuralist analysis of the plots – that the genre of the Western is divided into historically consecutive plot variants – is not lacking in interpretation and reflection, and Wright makes a serious attempt to analyse the relation between film and society.

Stories and their reception

The main methodic problem of the research approach discussed above is that it takes for granted the narrative structure and the structure of the collective consciousness that the narratives are supposed to reflect. In Wright's study, for instance, there are no viewers, no interpretations or accounts of how they have probed the mythical worlds of the Western. Yet Wright presents a far-reaching interpretation of the American collective consciousness and of how it has changed historically entirely on the basis of an analysis of Westerns. The only step he takes towards checking the link between the structures of the Westerns, on the one hand, and those of the collective conscious, on the other, is to restrict his sample of Westerns to the top grossing films of the year they were released. One may therefore assume that they appealed to the viewers.

Sharply critical of this decision, Janice Radway decided in her own work to include the people who knew the story, the consumers. *Reading the Romance* (Radway 1984) applies the methods of ethnographic research to a study of the readership of Harlequin romance books. The material for Radway's study consists of these paperbacks, but the analysis is also based on an ethnography and personal interviews of women who were in the habit of buying their romances at a particular bookstore. In the interviews, the women were asked to name the three best romances and romance writers. High-ranking stories and writers were then selected as the object of a narrative structural analysis. The same was done with the stories that the women considered as failures.

This was how Radway reached her conclusions about the meaning and function of the reading of romances to these women. According to Radway, reading romances is an expression of discontent with the lot of a housewife and at once a compensatory activity. Through the personages of the heroines and heroes, the readers explored the position of women and different ways in which they might organize it so that it better met their own desires. The heroines in the female-sponsored fantasies did not let themselves be treated as mere objects or men's servants; they rather had an active role both in society and in their love life. Reading romances was in a concrete sense a way of taking distance from the role of housewife, an opportunity temporarily to refuse to play the part of a person defined as a public resource to be mined at will by the family. On the other hand, the endings of the tales suggested that it is possible for a woman to arrange her life in a way that better meets with her utopias without radically changing the traditional position of women or the institutional foundation of gender relations. Reading romances is also a compensatory activity in the sense that it helps women tolerate the everyday life of a housewife, without their feeling a pressing urge to change it. However, Radway does not want to denounce the romances as mere conservative ideology. In the end, she says, we simply do not know what practical effects the repetitive reading of romances has, in the long run, on the way women behave. However, Radway believes that the most recent trends which have seen heroines become even more independent and intelligent and the heroes gentler and more expressive suggests that even romances do keep abreast of the times, possibly even change accustomed lines of thought.

The audience of stories can be taken into account, then, in the ethnographic method. One has to bear in mind that its weakness is the modest size of the 'sample'. One could, for instance, argue that Radway's results are completely invalid among another readership or its subgroups.

One way to go about this problem is to combine narrative analysis with statistical data describing the consumption of mass culture products. This is what was done in an analysis of the reception in Finland of a German detective television series that originally went by the name of *Der Alte* (see Alasuutari and Kytömäki 1986). The objective of the study was to explain why this police series, together with so-called high-brow films, was the most popular fiction programme among highly educated and upper middle-class TV-viewers. The solution of the problem was based on two findings.

Firstly, narrative analysis showed that the motive of the crime in *Der Alte* always stems from internal strictures within the nuclear family; in most cases the initial reason is infidelity. Other research has shown that these kinds of private problems are particularly well known to highly educated, go-ahead, two-career upper middle-class families.

The other explanation was based on a suggested symbolic homology between the role of the hero in classical detective stories and the job role of a person doing mental work. The classical detective story can be defined as a story where the hero – as well as the viewer or the reader – is trying to make inferences about what has happened or what is happening 'behind the scenes', unbeknownst to the hero and the viewer. To figure out the solution, the hero collects information and hints: clues that will help to resolve the mystery. The suspense ends as soon as the hero figures out the solution, most typically finds out who committed the murder. This kind of story differs radically from, say, a folk tale or a Western, where the villain of the narrative is known from the word go: there the action and the excitement is based on the fight between the villain and the hero. There are various intermediate forms that can be positioned in-between these extreme examples, story types which include both straight and backstage action. The link of these narrative types to work roles is obvious: the hero of the classical detective story is a white-collar worker, the action film hero corresponds symbolically to the manual labourer. On the basis of this theory we went on to formulate this hypothesis: the purer the classical detective story, the greater the proportion of white-collar workers in the audience, and vice versa: the more closely the programme resembles an action film, the smaller the proportion of white-collar workers in the audience. An empirical analysis of the audiences of various fictitious films and series supported the hypothesis: along with *Der Alte*, the most popular programmes among the upper middle-class viewers were some Agatha Christie films, the least popular were American action series such as *Matt Houston* and *Knight Rider*.

From product analysis to people's own stories

Even if the preferences of readers or spectators are taken into account in interpreting the results of narrative analysis, the kind of research setting discussed above still does not solve the problem that the 'narrative structure' itself is regarded as a given property that is thought to be incorporated into the cultural product. Yet a story is not constructed as a story until it is processed and interpreted by the recipient, and its structure is therefore also dependent on what goes on in the recipient's mind, on the individual's world-view and patterns of thought. This point has been made in a later trend of narrative analysis, often called the schema theory. Here it is pointed out that it is possible to understand a narrative only on the basis of what are called structures of expectation. Unlike Lévi-Straussian structuralism, where the structures of meaning are assumed to be inherent in various kinds of 'texts' and where these structures are given precedence over the subject who is producing the narrative to herself or himself, schema theory starts out from the interpreting subject and the act of reading. Consider the following fragment of a story:

> Mary heard the ice cream man coming down the road. She remembered her birthday money and rushed into the house. . . .

These few words are enough to provide us with a fairly complete interpretation of the events in the story. Mary is presumably a little girl who wants to buy an ice cream from the ice cream man and is therefore in a hurry to fetch her money from home. It does not literally say this in the story. One could also infer that Mary is afraid that the ice cream man might steal her birthday money. Still, most readers find the first interpretation plausible and will retain it unless contradicted by later information. In interpreting a narrative we apply a schema that best seems to make the story plausible. (Rumelhart 1977)

If people who represent different socio-economic groups or genders apply somewhat differing schemata in the interpretation of cultural products, it follows that the same story is different when interpreted by different people. If, by studying the reception of cultural products, we want to come to grips with the meaning structures or schemata that structure or guide people's thinking, surely it makes more sense to focus on people's interpretations rather than on the problematic 'stories as such'?

One way to study the interpreter's own reception is to ask people to recite the story in their own words. The researcher can then analyse the new, possibly tape-recorded stories, instead of studying the 'objective' structures of the 'original' story. This will also radically change the whole research setting. The starting-point is no longer the story, understood as a cultural product, the *reception* of which among the audience or its various subgroups would then be the research problem. Rather, the focal concern is with *the story produced to the self* or, to be precise, a story about a story. In an interview it becomes integrated into other self-expressions and discussions: a story among other stories, comments and evaluations. The 'object' interpreted by the audience is thus in its essence and external appearance similar to other talk of the interviewees. An interviewee's story about a programme she has seen or a tale she has read can be simply compared to the way she talks about her work, leisure interests or past, about various external objects as they are understood by her, and dressed in the form of a story.

The solution may seem less novel and strange if it is compared to the use of another type of data used as research material, i.e. life-stories. Life-stories, of course, are also about the subjects' own interpretations; interpretations that concern their own life cycles. The methods of narrative analysis can also be applied to the study of these life-stories (see Alasuutari 1986).

This comparison to life-stories also goes to show that accounts which chronicle personal experiences involve more or less all the same problems as were discussed earlier in connection with the meaning of cultural products. It is not that easy for the researcher to determine the 'narrative structure' or other 'essential' content of a life-story, as Vilkko (1988) has shown. There are many levels and layers in a story. First of all a life-story is an account about a *life that has been lived*, about certain living conditions and environments. Secondly, it is a *story* among other stories. In a life-story the subject talks about things that have happened, about choices that he or she as appearing in the story has made, assesses and criticizes those choices, as well as the subject who took those decisions as an individual and personality. In addition, in this sort of cultural product it is possible to analyse the style in which the account has been written, how the subject who is speaking addresses the implied reader, and advises the reader as to how the narrative should be understood (see also Lejeune 1989).

From cognitive structures to discourses

The kind of approach to life-stories or other forms of narrating or discussion outlined above opens a whole new can of worms recently tackled in discourse analysis. For instance, the schema theory assumes that talk and texts reflect or represent humans' cognitive structures, especially how knowledge is stored in hierarchical schemata, scripts and frames in the brain. However, different trends of discourse analysis show that frames or discourses have a much more context-bound character, and that language use is also part of social action: choices of words and discourses also have social consequences. Goffman (1974) uses the concept of frame in a slightly different manner. By frame, he refers to sets of rules that constitute activities so that they are defined as activities of a certain type. When in everyday life we form some picture of 'what is going on', we have located a frame that makes the situation (at least partially) understandable. Potter and Wetherell (1987, 146–157) refer to more or less the same idea by the concept of '*interpretative repertoires*'. The fact that individuals seem to talk in contradictory ways about a topic can be made understandable by analysing and identifying the different repertoires people employ in different contexts. They construct their objects in different ways, and their use serves different purposes.

Such repertoires or discourses are also thought to be linked with identity construction, but not as text-level evidence of individuals' innermost cognitive structures. Instead, discourses are thought of as representations with certain *subject positions* inscribed within them. Invoking and negotiating between different discourses within which to construct a situation is a form of constant everyday-life identity politics.

As to media or reception research, this 'constructionist' or 'discursive' perspective means a move away from a psychological and cognitive framework to a more sociological one. The discourses or repertoires interviewees use can be related to those prevalent in society, and also in media research itself. For instance, Radway's study of female romance readers is only understandable against the background that such mass cultural products are thought to be harmful for women's emancipation. Radway is opposed to that view, which Ien Ang (1985) has called the 'ideology of mass culture', but only within the same discourse: she partly justifies reading romances by showing that they may actually have emancipatory potential. However, it seems that the past decades have seen a gradual relaxation in the concerns for the harmful effects of mass culture. More recently Ang (1991) has placed this development in an institutional framework. According to her, the promotion of 'high culture' and 'quality television' can be seen as part of the public service ideal of educating the masses, and the legitimacy of that ideology is in crisis.

All in all, the discursive approach means a broadened frame within which to conceive of the media and media use. This does not necessarily mean abandoning ethnographic case studies of audiences or analyses of individual programmes, but the focus is not restricted to finding out about the reception or 'reading' of a programme by a particular audience. Rather, the objective is to get a grasp of our contemporary 'media culture', particularly as it can be seen in the role of the media in everyday life, both as a topic and as an activity structured by and structuring the discourses within which it is discussed (cf. Alasuutari forthcoming).

Method is part of the research setting

The shift from surveys or ethnographies to the analysis of cultural products has been one way of tackling the macro-structures of modern society; not, however, the underlying power or economic structures but its cultural structures. Nevertheless, it seems that the internal development of this approach has once again forced researchers to reassess their presuppositions. In the hands of critical researchers, the great structures and systems of society seem to become splintered into ever smaller units for separate analyses.

This trend from grand structuralist cosmological systems towards more and more detailed and individual reading of stories, story-telling situations and discourses may easily be seen as a story of the progress of science in which the plot is one of accumulating knowledge about the dilemmas embedded in the previous research designs. In this light the post-structuralist critique of Lévi-Straussian structuralism discussed in the previous chapter appears to be well founded. The interest that researchers have been showing in *langue*, the unobservable underlying structure of language (as opposed to *parole* as its outward manifestation), has been the latest, desperate attempt to find a solid, constant essence behind the instability of appearances. When everything else has failed, all that is left is a belief in the structure of language. This is how Derrida sees it (Rorty 1982, 90–109).

One might also perceive this development as part of the historical changes of Western society. The breakdown of collectivities into ever smaller groups and separate individuals erodes the foundation on which intersubjectivity rests as a confined and definable structure. Therefore microsociological considerations are also becoming of greater interest in the sphere of cultural studies.

It is for this reason that the methodic solutions outlined above cannot be rank-ordered. When methods change, so too do the research settings, and vice versa. In the studies discussed above, researchers have wanted to answer different questions and in terms of different theoretical frameworks. The 1980s and 1990s have witnessed a shift from structuralist and macrosociological research problems towards studies of subjectivity and identity. It is obvious that in a macrosociological framework the differences in the reception of cultural products between individuals and various social strata are inessential. Correspondingly, when studying life-styles and forms of identity by analysing the consumption of cultural products, we cannot be content with the researcher's own appraisal of the way individuals conceive the story.

The method is an essential part of the research setting because it helps the researcher to see the aspects that are most relevant from the vantage-point adopted. However, there is no research setting which can exempt the researcher from submitting an interpretation, a logical idea of what can be said about the subject on the basis of the material collected and the conceptual and methodic system applied to analysing that material. It is important to make one's case as convincingly as one can, to prove the validity of one's explanatory model – but of course it also has to be borne in mind that the conclusion is never a hard fact and actually no more than the best guess.

CHAPTER 9

FROM SURVEYS TO IN-DEPTH INTERVIEWS AND CONVERSATIONS

From interviews to dialogue as action

There are probably two big differences between the natural and the social sciences. One is of course that the natural sciences study mechanics and processes as they occur unaffected by human interference, whereas the social sciences concentrate on human action – without being able to disregard the natural processes that condition it. The other main difference is that the objects of the natural sciences cannot be asked questions. Metaphorically it is often said that the scientist poses questions to reality, but in fact only humans can talk back.

It is hardly surprising, then, that the ancient method of interviewing has been an important part of social research. Much of the history of the social sciences could be written as a story about the development of different uses of and perspectives on conversation both as a method and as part of the social reality being studied.

The same could be said of detective stories. In detective stories you can find examples of practically all possible approaches to conversation from police cross-examinations to casual chit-chat without any apparent function in solving the case.

When we think about conversations as a research tool, gathering facts about the object or event under scrutiny by asking questions is a self-evident example. Consider an extract from the Conan Doyle story 'The Norwood Builder', in which a client, John Hector McFarlane, comes to Sherlock Holmes because he is suspected of murdering Mr Oldacre:

> 'Mr Oldacre had told me that he would like me to have supper with him at nine, as he might not be home before that hour. I had some difficulty in finding his house, however, and it was nearly half-past before I reached it.
>
> I found him–'
>
> 'One moment!' said Holmes. 'Who opened the door?'
>
> 'A middle-aged woman, who was, I suppose, his house-keeper.'
>
> 'And it was she, I presume, who mentioned your name?'
>
> 'Exactly,' said McFarlane.
>
> 'Pray proceed.'

In the extract above, Sherlock Holmes uses interviewing as a way of accessing events which he has not witnessed. During the interview he pictures the unfolding of events in his mind's eye, and with his unrivalled wit he is shown to realize details that the witnesses themselves may have failed to notice or pay attention to. In such cases he interrupts the witness to get the missing pieces of information. This is quite typical of Conan Doyle, for whom dialogue is clearly secondary to figuring out a mystery considered as a chain of events. The interview is used as a method of data collection, by which the hero sheds light on those events. Elsewhere (Alasuutari 1995, 47–62) I have called this view on interviews and speech the *factist* perspective. This perspective looks upon language merely as a channel through which information about reality is conveyed. The context in which the conversation takes place or the particular forms or words used are ignored, unless they are considered as potential signs of the informants' untrustworthiness or dishonesty.

For many later detective authors, dialogue and interviews have many other functions besides that of gathering facts. For instance, they contribute to the picture that is drawn of the main characters to the reader: how they relate to other people, and to questions such as love and romance or life and death. In many cases the heroes solving a murder case also approach interviews and dialogues from this viewpoint: to form a 'psychological profile' of the possible suspects. Besides, the hero of a crime story may use dialogue as a weapon to 'stir things up', to make interventions in an unknown web of interpersonal relations and thus learn more about it.

Consider an episode from Ross MacDonald's story *The Way Some People Die*. The private detective Lew Archer discovers that Galley, the young woman he is trying to find, is kept imprisoned by a crook, Mr Dowser, who wants to force her to tell him where her husband is. To find out more about the whole constellation, Archer pretends to help Dowser make her talk:

> '. . . But here's my idea. The girl has a notion I might be on her side.' If Galley had that notion, she was right. 'If you muss my hair and shove me in alongside her, it should convince her. I suppose you've got her locked in some dungeon?'

To convince Dowser, Archer even takes money from him, promising to himself that at the earliest opportunity he will bet it on the horses. In the lockup Archer then talks with Galley, knowing that Dowser has bugged the room so that he can hear the conversation. Aside from the task of making her tell him where Joe, her husband, a petty crook who has betrayed Dowser, might have gone, Archer doesn't really know what he is looking for:

> 'So you married Joe, who probably shot Speed himself.' I made the suggestion at random, fishing for facts.

In this example the function of conversations is quite complicated. It is not simply a matter of what individuals say and whether what they say is trustworthy or not. The investigator has to ask why individuals react the way they do to questions, claims or suggestions made by the investigator or by others appearing in different roles and positions. The investigator does not try to remain neutral or detached from the researched events to get 'objective' accounts from the interviewees. Instead, in this approach to interviews and conversations we regard any reaction or response in human interaction in its context. What can we infer from the fact that in this particular context a participant reacted in a particular way to a particular 'prod', whatever it is? Elsewhere (Alasuutari 1995, 85–100), I have called this the *interaction* perspective. In it, the investigator's role is not one of a neutral inquirer gathering true statements, but rather one of a person who by entering the field and asking questions necessarily makes an intervention and 'pushes' people to react, thus learning about the culture and social reality he or she is studying. Even in a conventional interview, the role of the investigator is that of an active interviewer (Holstein and Gubrium 1995).

In Dashiell Hammett's stories the 'partisan' role of the investigator sometimes goes even further. The detective turns into an adventurer who has no time to solve mysteries but who just wants to win a battle or at least stay alive. The background of the events in the midst of which the hero finds himself is often revealed only afterwards. The only real reminder of the genre of detective stories is the cool analytic attitude with which, for instance, the Continental Op weighs how to play his cards the best possible way. In *The House in Turk Street*, the Op tries to play the crooks against each other:

'I got him, Tai,' she called, and the Chinese joined us.
   'What did Hook do with the bonds?' he asked point blank.
   I grinned into his round yellow face and led my ace.
   'Why don't you ask the girl?'
   His face showed nothing, but I imagined that his fat body stiffened a little within its fashionable British clothing. That encouraged me, and I went on with my little lie that was meant to stir things up.
   'Haven't you rapped to it,' I asked, 'that they were fixing up to ditch you?'
   'You dirty liar!' the girl screamed, and took a step toward me.

This kind of partisan role as an investigator and as a person who not only or even primarily wants to solve a case but instead tries to 'make things right' could be paralleled to action research, as was done in Chapter 6. However, the move away from describing an interviewer-researcher to that of an 'action researcher' could just as well be compared to the discovery made in the social sciences that language is also action: that turns of talk in a social situation can be viewed as 'speech acts' (Austin 1962; Searle 1976). Every expression can be examined from the point of view not only of its meaning but also its effects. For example, when a priest at a wedding ceremony declares the couple husband and wife, he will be producing a new state of affairs. In the genre of detective stories, the acknowledgement of this aspect of language led to a more active detective role, whereas in social research it led to a problematization of the role of the interviewer and the interview situation. It also led to approaches such as discourse analysis and conversation analysis, where one is not so much interested in the information content of talk in a situation as in the conversation in its own right: how turns of talk can be seen like moves in a game, continuously changing the situation and redefining the positions and identities of the participants.

From informants to respondents

In social research the use of interviews in gathering information from a researched population has gone by the name of survey. However, it took quite a long time for the modern survey methodology to develop and to be institutionalized. Now that the survey is an important part of empirical social research, its interviewing strategy seems self-evident. Yet it was not until the 1920s that the statistical survey was established as a paradigm. This mystery, the non-establishment of the modern survey, has fascinated researchers so much that a great deal of the sociology of social science deals with this problem (Kent 1981; Oberschall 1965; Selvin 1985).

Why was it so difficult to invent the survey interviewing strategy? One reason is probably the indirect way in which survey research addresses its questions. In this light, the idea of early surveys to directly ask informed citizens to provide answers to the research problems seems much more natural. It comes much closer to the use of language for informative purposes in everyday life. This is why it was also natural that the questions were posed to knowledgeable citizens, such as state officials or church ministers. In other words, they were informants in *expert interviews*. For instance, in a survey of agricultural labourers conducted in 1874–1875 in Germany (Oberschall 1965, 19–20), question No. 25 read: 'Is there a tendency among laborers to save money in order to be able to buy their own plot of land later on? Does this tendency appear already among the unmarried workers or only after marriage?'

The modern survey would of course approach such questions quite differently. Instead of asking an informed person whether married or unmarried workers have a tendency to save money to buy their own plot of land, a sample of workers would be asked about their marital status, savings, and plans about how to use them. The study subjects are not told why this or that question is actually asked, and survey methodology expressly disregards individuals' own 'sociological imagination', even when it comes to assessing their own action. Yet respondents are supposed to give honest answers. To put it briefly, the survey interview is a fairly peculiar institution when compared with ordinary conversations and more traditional ways of gathering information by asking people.

The form that interviewing was to assume in the modern survey not only enabled the use of statistics in the analysis of interview data. It also had the effect of distancing the researcher and the respondent from the frame of an ordinary conversation, and that was interpreted to mean that the social survey is a truly scientific research method.

Indeed, the survey questionnaire gives an air of natural science research to what essentially is asking people questions. It has neutrally framed questions and preset response options, often presented in terms of a scale. One would ask, for instance: 'Are you (1) very satisfied, (2) satisfied, (3) indifferent, (4) dissatisfied or (5) very dissatisfied with your job?' Social researchers even started talking about the results of such questions as 'measuring' things like 'job satisfaction', as if they were physical objects rather than linguistic constructs, and as if the data were not acquired through the use of natural language, by individuals giving answers. In survey research the essential role of language in data collection, the fact that makes social research different from natural science, is in this way often pushed aside. Questions and answers are treated as if they were measuring instruments and measurement results.

The survey interview or self-administered questionnaire is certainly in many ways an unusual form of interaction. That does not, however, mean it is inevitably inhuman and unacceptable as such. It is just another language game that people easily learn to play; a game whose rules of interaction differ from those applied in ordinary conversations.

For the interviewer the rules of this game set certain requirements (see, e.g., Fink 1995). The questions must be neutrally worded, conventional language, which is easy to understand and does not arouse strong emotions and connotations in an uncontrolled and unpredictable way. Fink (ibid., 28) talks about 'biasing' words and phrases. Unless one is studying a homogeneous group who share a special language, slang and colloquialisms must be avoided. Two-edged questions must be avoided: each question should contain only one idea.

In one sense the survey seems quite easy for the surveyor, for the person who actually goes out and asks people questions. That is because everything taking place in the interaction situation is or should be carefully planned in advance, and not much else should be said during the actual interview situation than what is printed on the questionnaire and on the surveyor's instructions about how to introduce the survey and how to conduct the interview.

However, that is so only in theory. Although the questionnaires must be pretested, there will always be questions that not all people quite understand, or they will want to know why a question has been asked: what exactly are the researchers after? The respondents may also consult the surveyor about the right answer option by explaining their particular situation. On the other hand, the surveyors may not want to spend too much time on a single interview. Therefore, if a person stops to think about the right option to an answer, the surveyors may propose an answer which in their experience would be the option others have chosen in a similar case.

Theoretically, all this negotiation about the answers is forbidden, because it does not take place the same way in each interview, and there are personal differences between interviewers. However, in actual practice one could not even in theory eliminate the elements of human interaction present in the filling of a questionnaire. The problems of conducting the interview are not restricted to solving how to react to respondents' requests for clarification about the questions asked. More generally we are talking about the whole way of indeed *conducting* an interaction situation. The interviewers, for instance, have to decide how they present themselves in relation to the research. In leading the respondent to the next question, does the interviewer, for instance, say that 'we' or 'they' would like the respondent to answer a question? What if a respondent criticizes a question or its preset options: do the surveyors try to defend the questionnaire, acknowledge a weakness, or dis-associate themselves from the research with the attitude, 'I don't know, I just work here'?

These are probably not 'either–or' choices that could be decided beforehand. A survey interview, or any interview for that matter, is like a theatre piece in which only one actor has part of his or her lines written down. This special actor has the task of finalizing a draft into a play, which includes act one with an introduction, the act containing the interview itself, and an act with more informal conversation, perhaps a cup of coffee served by the respondent. Moreover, the individuals appearing in the special role of the surveyor have to make the respondents choose their lines from a limited list of options, and to prepare themselves how to respond to any improvisation on the part of the respondent, so that the dialogue is brought back to the questionnaire serving as the manuscript draft. The order of the acts and the partly improvised parts in the dialogue vary from performance to performance, because the role of the respondent is each time filled with a new actor, with no prior information about the contents of the interview and often with no previous personal experience of any survey interviews. First interviews are like rehearsals for the surveyor, but with practice and interviewing experience the filling of the particular question-naire develops into a play that goes smoothly, almost regardless of what happens during a single interview.

By describing the survey interview as a language game and a theatre play I do not mean to say that the *reliability* of survey data is unavoidably poor: that the results are totally random because they are based on choices made by individuals under 'biased' circumstances. In most cases another similar sample of respondents would produce the same breakdown of answer options, and in that sense the results are reliable. There are no unbiased circumstances; it is only a matter of how well we are able to take the conditions of data collection into account and thus to leap 'beyond' them.

The influence of, say, the personality or gender of the inter-viewer can be controlled for, and in most cases it can be convincingly shown that the answers people give to the questions are far from being simply functions of the interaction situation, or even contingent on the particular human interactive form that the filling of the questionnaire had assumed. Besides, one must bear in mind that, unlike in public opinion polls, in proper survey analysis one is not normally interested in how many people have chosen a particular answering option to a single question. Instead, one is interested in the probability with which the respondents' choices of certain options are associated with particular choices in answering some other questions.

Since surveys do produce statistical relations between answer options, relations that hold through the data, they reflect differences between individual respondents' preferences in answering the questions. It is only by paying attention to the filling in of a survey questionnaire as a form of interaction that we are able to better assess the *validity* of the research results. Ordinarily, validity is defined as the extent to which a method, measure or an indicator is thought to measure what it sets out to measure, but it could just as well be said that we are dealing with our ability to make sense of the findings. We should be able to know the meaning of the statistical relations: what are the phenomena underlying the fact that certain variables correlate with each other?

The seriousness of the validity problem in survey research depends on the variables in question. At one extreme there are survey analysis results which more or less reproduce the statistical relations between variables found in population data: how education is associated with income level, or how gender is associated with occupation. In such analyses it may be quite safely assumed that the interview situation is not an important intervening factor in explaining the correlations found. The problems start at the point where individuals are asked about their attitudes or requested to describe their behaviour. The standard survey research report language treats the answers as 'behaviour' or 'attitudes' themselves, as if they were solid, easily measurable objects, totally stripped of the contingencies of the answering situation. This creates greater problems for validity.

For instance, how do we know how respondents, or different subsets of respondents, have understood the questions, or

rather how have they interpreted the meaning of asking particular questions? In surveys, researchers will typically try to
control for validity by keeping the respondents 'in the dark'
about the function of different questions. It is assumed that
the respondents just naïvely and honestly respond, without
speculating on what the researcher is after. In reality, however,
people do not answer a single question without in some way
interpreting its sense and meaning.

In the modern times of 'opinion poll democracy', marketing
research, psychological tests and, indeed, social surveys, the
'survey interview' itself forms a general frame with which
citizens are quite familiar. Within this frame they think it is only
natural for surveyors to ask about their occupation, education,
income, and all sorts of questions. This means that they more or
less know why these questions are being asked, and how the
data will be analysed and presented as research results.
Although often only half of the individuals in a survey sample
respond, it can be said that answering survey questions is based
on a general trust in empirical social research; a trust that was
still missing in the nineteenth century and early twentieth
century, when workers often *en masse* refused to take part in the
first surveys. Now it is believed that surveys contribute to the
betterment of society, or at least they do no harm. For instance,
opinion polls are viewed as a kind of extension to the democratic
vote.

However, the fact that one is responding to a survey is not a
sufficient interpretive frame for answering questions. Different
questions evoke different frames within which answers are
given, and they may also vary from one individual and population group to another. People give their answers in terms of
those frames. Also, because people believe that surveys may
serve them or society at large, for instance by sending a
message to the decision-makers, they may respond in ways
which best serve their interests.

Answering survey questions is also a form of self-
presentation, and reflects an individual self-image and social
identity. Even if one wants to give honest answers, it is often
quite difficult to assess how much time one spends on different
tasks on the job, on watching television and different programmes, or on household chores. So the question is: to what
extent do the results reflect actual behaviour, or do they rather

reflect individuals' attempts to be consistent with their self-image? As regards questions about individual attitudes, it is hard to know whether people really think the way they claim to, or whether they are expressing attitudes which they believe are politically correct or appropriate for persons in their social standing.

As has been noted, one of the few strategies in trying to avoid these problems of validity in survey research is that researchers try their best to conceal the purpose of different questions. Psychological tests, with, for instance, different drawing tasks or instructions to immediately say what a word or other stimulus brings to mind, are perhaps farthest advanced in this 'armaments race'. Yet even the proper responses to ever new psychological test questions soon become part of folklore: individuals are trained to do well in those tests as part of job interviews, for instance.

Controlling for different intervening variables and cross-checking the information gained by asking the same questions in different ways are other strategies of trying to cope with the survey's validity. However, since much of the 'bias' in survey answers stems from the respondents' attempt to be consistent with their self-image and social identity, that does not necessarily help.

Concealing the real purpose of survey questions gives rise to ethical problems (see Eskola 1988). However, a more profound problem is that such things as interpretive frames or self-images are treated as sources of bias, instead of being considered as an essential part of what human reality and interaction are all about.

In-depth interviews

Within the social sciences from the 1960s onwards, the problems of survey methodology outlined above have led to the re-discovery and renaissance of open-ended interviews and qualitative interviewing more generally. Several researchers coming from different traditions have argued that structured survey interviews are too restricting and unnatural. It has been argued that more informal interviews are the way to get 'deeper', to learn what things mean to the study subjects.

To find out why people behave the way they do, Harré and Secord (1972) simply suggested, 'Why not ask them?' They also crystallized their *ethogenic* approach in an ironic way by demanding that, 'for scientific purposes, people should be treated as if they were human beings', thus capable of giving accounts of their behaviour.

In actual research practice this approach means that, in addition to perhaps observing individuals in their natural environments, in interviews one is interested in people's own accounts of their behaviour, because they are assumed to reveal the rules people follow and thus the meaning of the action in question.

> At the heart of the explanation of social behaviour is the identification of the meanings that underlie it. Part of the approach to discovering them involves the obtaining of *accounts* – the actor's own statements about why he performed the acts in question, what social meanings he gave to the actions of himself and others. These must be collected and analysed, often leading to the discovery of the rules that underlie the behaviour. (ibid., 9)

In the ethogenic approach one acknowledges that accounts and behaviour are two different things, and that giving accounts serves its own function in relation to action, but it is asserted that action and accounting depend on the same 'stock of social knowledge' that can be studied by collecting and analysing accounts:

> The fundamental ethogenic hypothesis that links acting and accounting is the idea that an individual's ability to do either depends upon his stock of social knowledge. Such knowledge forms a single system in each individual person so that his actions and accounts are performances drawing only upon one corpus of knowledge. This knowledge is revealed in different ways of acting and in accounting since each is directed to a different end. Actions are the means by which we accomplish social acts, while accounts serve to make what we do intelligible and justified. Our studies are aimed at revealing this knowledge and exploring its structure. (Marsh et al. 1978, 15)

Marsh et al.'s (1978) study of 'trouble-makers' in schools and at football matches is an empirical example of the ethogenic approach. They observed the young people's action in natural settings at football stadiums, and even recorded it in video and audio form. Complementary to that record they collected accounts given by those fans of those same occasions and others like them. In the other case study of occasions of violence in schools they only had the accounts. Such accounts were then renegotiated, and were the subject of much discussion between the fans and the researchers (ibid., 23). Let us take an excerpt from an interview:

> *Interviewer*: Why are there people fighting in the first place at some games. What's your explanation?
> *Mike*: Well – I suppose if there's enough of you the idea is sort of to take the other team's End.
> *Interviewer*: For what reason?
> *Mike*: Well it's something to boast about.
> [. . .]
> *George*: When you get some of the other side's fans in your End – that's when the trouble really starts. It's your territory – your property – it's like someone just walking into your house or something like that. Well you just have to get them out one way or another. You can't stand for that. (ibid., 103–104)

According to the researchers' interpretation based on the participants' accounts, fans perceive fights as having a particular kind of structure to them. For instance, 'territorial invasion constitutes a legitimation of attack' (ibid., 105). Moreover, if individuals are challenged by staring, or 'screwing' as the fans call it, or if someone is called a 'cunt', the persons to whom the challenge is directed 'must respond or risk the possibility of losing face' (ibid., 106).

As can be seen, in this interviewing strategy the idea is to negotiate an explanation that is internally consistent and in accordance with other facts, such as observations about the action in question. The end result is a formulation of a rule or a set of rules which describe the meaning of the action for the people, and which thus make the action understandable.

For ethogenics the concept of meaning refers primarily to the meaning of action, but often in qualitative interviews one is interested more generally in the lived world of the subjects and their relation to it. As Kvale (1996, 31) puts it:

> The qualitative research interview seeks to describe and understand the meanings of central themes in the life world of the subjects. The main task in interviewing is to understand the meaning of what the interviewees say.

Kvale also maintains that a qualitative research interview seeks to cover both a factual and a meaning level. According to him, the latter means that it is necessary to listen to the explicit descriptions and meanings as well as to what is 'said between the lines'. This entails a negotiation of the meaning between the interviewer and interviewee: 'The interviewer may seek to formulate the "implicit message", "send it back" to the subject, and obtain an immediate confirmation or disconfirmation of the interviewer's interpretation of what the interviewee is saying' (ibid., 32).

The qualitative 'in-depth' interview is in many ways different from the survey interview. The main difference is of course that in qualitative interviews the questions are open-ended, and they have not been formulated prior to the interview session. The interviewer does normally have a check-list of themes to be covered in the interviews, but a great deal of the conversation consists of follow-up questions to what the interviewees say in the first place.

Different steps are also taken to try to improve the validity of data by different means. In survey methodology the aim is to avoid the 'reactivity of measurement' (Bernard 1988, 150; Dooley 1990, 106) – that is, the fact that the act of gathering information by bothering people with questions or other requests affects the information actually received. The interviewees or study subjects are often given limited information about the purpose of the study. The subjects are, for instance, not told told why the particular questions are asked. The method of improving validity could be called *mechanistic* (see Alasuutari 1995, 50–56). In the in-depth interview, by contrast, the strategy adopted in trying to improve the validity of the information gained is to be open and try to win the confidence of the informants. The key concept of this *humanistic* method (ibid., 50–53, 56–60) is 'rapport' (Berg 1989, 29–30; Bogdan and

Taylor 1975, 45–48; Georges and Jones 1980, 63–64). It is thought that if the researcher makes friends with the informants, and if the informants trust the researcher, they will also be honest with him or her.

There are also features of the therapeutic interview in the in-depth interview. When interviewee and interviewer become 'peers' or 'companions' (Reason and Rowan 1981, 205), and discuss the meaning of different aspects of the subject's life perhaps on several interview occasions, they reach an internal truth. Kvale (1996, 34) says that in the course of an interview subjects may change their descriptions of, and meanings about, a theme: 'The subjects may themselves have discovered new aspects of the themes they are describing, and suddenly see relations that they had not been conscious of earlier.'

The 'therapeutic aspect' of the in-depth interview is evident in the fact that the interview itself is seen as the first step of analysis. In this step, the interviewer, during the interview, condenses and interprets the meaning of what the interviewee describes. The interviewing implies an ongoing 'on-the-line-interpretation' with the possibility of confirmation or discon-firmation of the interviewer's interpretations (Kvale 1996, 189).

However, there are also similarities between the survey interview and the in-depth interview. In the latter, one also presumes that there are true and honest answers to the ques-tions posed. The problem of validity boils down to the problem of honesty and truthfulness on the side of the interviewees. In surveys, one is normally interested in the external facts of the respondent's life, whereas in the in-depth interview we are concerned with the 'internal' reality of the subjects: how do they perceive reality, and what are the real meanings of differ-ent aspects of their life-world? Although the in-depth interview researcher is more interested in the language people use, it is still regarded as a channel through which the truth about their inner and outer reality is communicated. In that sense the in-depth interview is a variant of the factist perspective.

The discursive interview

Recently, a somewhat different approach has been taken towards qualitative interviews, especially to the material produced. The so-called 'linguistic turn' has called into question the notion of truth that can be achieved through interviewing. This is not the same as to argue that one cannot make a difference between more or less substantiated inferences about interview data; that all interpretations are equally valid or subjective. The point is just that one cannot simply equate individuals' accounts and interview talk with their 'life-world' or what things 'mean' to them. Instead, within a discursive approach to interview data one first and foremost considers interviews as a particular kind of talk-in-interaction, a social institution in its own right. Then, within this basic framework, there are various ways in which to ask what the interview data tell about other reality: when people in this instance behave the way they do, what inferences can be drawn on that basis about their life and about social reality more generally? In this approach to interviewing, we treat the interview as a way of producing an interaction situation and different forms and aspects of discourse invoked in it.

What is here called the discursive interview is in effect more a perspective on qualitative interview data than a particular interviewing strategy. Any interviews, even tape-recorded or video-taped survey interviews, can be approached from this perspective, as specimens (cf. Alasuutari 1995, 63) of talk-in-interaction. However, the discursive perspective does have implications for the interviewing technique. We are not interested in the information and descriptions provided by respondents, but rather treat interviews as a means to gather specimens of talk in different contexts, as a way to make people (including the interviewer) produce research material for subsequent analysis. That is why the interviewing strategies differ from those advocated by proponents of the in-depth interview.

In the discursive interview one is often interested in collecting a plethora of discourses within which people deal with a topic. One of the problems in doing this by means of interviewing is the same as in the case of questionnaire studies: what one gets is conditioned by the interview context and by the questions asked, for instance by the concepts and frameworks provided by the interviewer. It is of course true that interviews can never be thought of as providing a direct access to the interviewees' world. The particular material produced would not even exist without the practice of doing interviews, and it is always co-produced by the interviewer and the respondent.

Yet there are marked differences in the degree to which the conversation is dominated by the interviewer. We can avoid 'feeding' the interviewees the concepts and frames within which to talk about a topic, and remain at a fairly abstract level as to the choice of words. A question like 'Tell me about your work' leaves it up to the interviewee to choose the concepts within which to give an account, and the interviewer can then take up the concepts the respondent has introduced in the follow-up questions. In them, instead of asking 'What do you mean by that?', you might ask for an example.

Concrete examples always produce interesting material, for several reasons. The question about a 'typical working day' probably produces accounts that represent individuals' self-reflexive frames within which to talk about their work, whereas 'Tell me about yesterday at work' may make the respondents describe events that for some reason do not belong to their stereotypical notion of their work. On the other hand, 'mini-stories' and 'anecdotes' provide examples of culturally crystal-lized story forms which are relatively independent from the particular context in which they are told.

In designing an interviewing strategy, one must always ask 'What do I ask the respondents to tell, so that the narratives they produce will shed light on the questions asked in the study?' Different kinds of questioning produce talk at different levels of reflexivity and from different narrative positions. For instance, to answer a direct question about how an interviewee perceives a problem in his or her life requires a lot of self-reflection, and probably makes the respondent move at the level of, and weigh between, reasons one commonly gives to the problem in question: what would best explain their problems, and is it socially acceptable to admit them? That is all inter-esting material for anyone who wants to study the discourses surrounding a problem, but a more personal question opens other discourses. You might, for instance, ask: 'Imagine that in five years' time the problem has disappeared (or worsened). What has happened? Such a hypothetical question makes people address their problems at a more concrete and personal level, thus allowing the researcher to see whether the under-lying discourses are different.

Let us take another example. Consider that you ask parents to say what in their view is the role and task of school in the child's development. The answers will probably list socially acceptable values, such as personality development, creativity or good manners. The question 'What would make you change your child to another school?' would probably produce quite different answers.

The relevant interviewing strategy depends on what we are after. If, for instance, the idea is to ask a person to tell his or her life-story, one will usually first ask people to tell their life-story in their own words, and the interviewer's task is to ask for more details by posing further questions about the episodes already taken up by the interviewee (see Alasuutari 1992, 57–84).

Holstein and Gubrium (1995) formulate the strategy of discursive interviewing by talking about active interviewing, by which they refer both to the interviewer and to the interviewee. According to them, active interviewing is a form of interpretive practice involving respondent and interviewer as they articulate ongoing interpretive structures, resources and orientations. Their active conception of the interview invests the subject with a substantial repertoire of interpretive methods and stock of experiential methods, and the interviewer's task is to incite a rich production of meanings that address issues relating to particular research concerns.

> With the interviewer's help, the respondent activates different aspects of his or her stock of knowledge, which we can hear in the conversational give-and-take of the interview. In the course of many open-ended interviews, for example, respondents intersperse their responses to interview items with telltale phrases such as 'speaking as a mother,' 'thinking like a woman,' 'if I were in her shoes,' 'after I heard what he said,' 'wearing my professional hat,' 'on second thought,' 'when you bother to think about it,' 'now that you ask,' 'I'm not sure about that one,' and 'I haven't really thought about it.' (ibid., 33)

It can be argued that this kind of active interviewing strategy, in which the respondent is asked to consider the topics discussed from different viewpoints, is biased by the interviewer's active role in suggesting such viewpoints and narrative positions. Holstein and Gubrium, however, rightly point out that 'any interview situation – no matter how formalized, restricted, or standardized – relies on the interaction between interview participants.'

From the viewpoint of treating the recorded interviews as research material in its own right, as a specimen of a particular talk-in-interaction, there are no 'biased' interviews. Any possible biases lie in the inferences about other reality drawn from the data. Consider an example from Sue Widdicombe and Robin Wooffitt's (1995) study of youth subculture members talking about their lives and identities. In the extract, the speaker gives an account of how he developed a particular musical taste:

I: When and how did you get inta being a rocker?
R: it must have been when I was about fourteen or fifteen
     (.)
     some friends at school were (.)
I: mmhm
R: an they- an I said oh heavy metal's rubbish, they said nah it's
     not an they gave me some tapes to listen an I did enjoy it,
     did ⌈like it
I: ⌊mmhm
R: and that's when I s-sort of started getting into it
     (.)
     before I sort of liked things like Duran Duran and Spandau
     Ballet (.) huh hh
I: mmhm and then I ⌈mean how-
R: ⌊but that's cos I hadn't heard heavy metal
     you see
     (ibid., 140–141, cited in Potter 1996, 126)

In this extract, the respondent invokes and disqualifies the initial expectation that he became a rocker because of peer pressure; an expectation that would threaten his *authentic* rocker identity. Potter (1996, 125) uses the extract as an example of what he calls *stake inoculation*: descriptions are constructed to head off the imputation of stake or interest. Such inoculations work by countering the potential of what are considered self-evident interpretations of why people behaved the way they did, for instance that a person has failed to transcend familiar stereotypes.

Tannen (1993) discusses the same phenomenon at a more general level by referring to *structures of expectation*. When giving an account, people automatically take into account what they consider as shared frames. For instance, if an account follows certain structures of expectation, the narrator may omit details which are in accordance with them. In that sense structures of expectation define what is relevant to say and what goes without saying. On the other hand, to make a point the speaker may invoke and build a frame just in order to break away from the initial expectation.

This opens up a particular perspective to analysing oral narratives, for instance, because there are particular repeatedly used linguistic 'devices' which mark denials of expectations. Tannen has shown that the word 'but', for example, is often used to mark the denial of an expectation not only of the preceding clause but of an entire preceding set of statements or of narrative coherence in general. An account of a film showed to a study subject provides an example:

> . . . sitting . . . and-- indeed (he) didn't sit in his seat, . . . but (he) sat-- m-- way up front on the bicycle. (ibid., 45)

In the extract, the bike-riding frame would lead one to assume that a boy sits on the seat of his bike, and that is why the narrator points to a departure from the frame by emphasizing that the boy did not sit on the seat.

In these examples, the interview or other text materials are approached as specimens of realities in their own right. The idea is not to treat the interviewees' talk as information given about the described object, as we would normally do when listening to someone. Instead, by making use of different methods such as semiotics, narrative analysis, rhetoric or different forms of discourse analysis, we make observations about the interview data as a whole. What is going on in the interview text and in the interaction situation? How do the participants (the interviewer and the interviewee) co-construct and negotiate their roles, definitions of the situation, or different objects of talk? What frames, discourses, 'interpretative repertoires' (Potter and Wetherell 1987) are invoked, and what functions do they serve? These are the kind of questions one asks the data at this point.

The next step is to infer how the interview material helps to address the questions posed in the study. The question asked at this point is: what does it tell us about the topic we are interested in that the data show evidence of these or those phenomena? In the case of the example above about 'stake inoculation', what does it tell us about the youth cultural group that the respondent wants to disqualify the interpretation that he became a rocker because of social pressure, and presents a story of how he came to like heavy metal because of the music itself? Is this a recurring feature in the interview and other materials? What other values apart from authentic rocker identity are invoked by the respondents? More generally, what are the different discourses or interpretative repertoires within which respondents represent rockers and personhood generally, and how are they linked to each other?

On the basis of the emphasis on authentic rocker identity, we do not have to assume that the respondent is telling the truth, that he indeed initially disliked heavy metal. That may or may not be true, but a more safe interpretation would be that the person places a positive value on an authentic rocker identity and rejects the image of a person influenced by social pressure.

However, that does not necessarily mean that the rockers always insist on their authenticity. Within another discourse authenticity may not be an issue at all. Such apparent contradictions in the respondents' speech can then be explained by the contexts in which the different discourses are invoked, and by the functions they serve. It is only at this level that we can make sense of the group's identity construction.

Analysis of the interview data should not be restricted only to the respondent's statements. We must also be reflective of the interviewer's and researcher's role. What are the taken-for-granted frames built into the research setting, in the questions the researcher poses in the interviews, and in the reactions to the interviewees' accounts? What insights can be gained about the researched phenomena in a broader framework?

Such questions may lead to collecting other relevant research material. For instance, does other readily available material show evidence of the same discourses as those found in the interviews?

Conversation analysis

Recent developments in qualitative methods have tended to shift the research attention away from interviews and towards all manner of naturally occurring data. Apart from easy and 'unobtrusive' access to such data, one major advantage is that naturally occurring data are specimens of language use in society in natural settings. In contrast to the situation with interview data, the institutional contexts of those data are known exactly. There is no need to indirectly infer the relationship of discourses and interaction situations to other reality.

When we are talking about spoken language – which is also what qualitative research interviews represent – this means that the concern is with conversations in natural settings (which can mean, for instance, news interviews). Ethnomethodological conversation analysis (CA) has offered many new insights for such research.

To put it briefly, the idea of CA is to analyse how conversationalists co-produce a shared understanding of what is going on in a conversation. What kinds of activities does conversation include? What kinds of structures do 'speech acts' exhibit? How do the people involved in the conversation produce an intersubjective conception of what they are doing? These are some of the more general questions that are addressed in CA. In a crude description one might say that this line of inquiry is interested in how the conversation moves from one turn to the next.

CA approaches language use from a 'speech-act' viewpoint in the sense that it is not so much interested in what is said as in what consequences it has for the course of interaction. How, for instance, does a previous turn of talk open and close options for the next turn, and how does that for its part define (but not *determine*) what takes place next in the interaction? For the parties involved in the conversation these structures are normative standards in the sense that they will orient themselves to interaction situations according to those rules and standards (Heritage 1984, 247–248; Nofsinger 1991, 53–54). If someone deviates from the rules, he or she will be expected to provide some sort of account of the reasons why. An example is provided by the common question–answer sequence of conversations. If you fail to answer a question within a reasonable space of time, the question will be repeated or you will be expected to give an account for not answering. The same applies to an invitation: whoever presented the invitation will assume that in reply you will either accept it or turn it down.

In CA, the researcher does not and should not try to guess whether an utterance was really meant as an invitation. The focus of analysis is restricted to those observations that are available to all participants in the conversation: to the information that is contained within the conversation itself. In other words, whether an utterance is named an 'invitation' or, for instance, a question depends on how the other party responds to it. Consider the following brief excerpt from a conversation (Atkinson and Drew, 1979, 58):

B: Why don't you come up and <u>see</u> me some [times
A: [I would like to

In expressing her consent, A is indicating that she has regarded what B said as an invitation. In other words we have here an *adjacency pair*: an invitation and its acceptance (unless A continues her turn of speech by 'but', which then leads to a polite refusal). If, on the other hand, A had taken B's turn of speech as a question and answered it, we would have had another adjacency pair: a question–answer pair. If, in the latter alternative, B had in fact intended her statement as an invitation and therefore not immediately received an appropriate answer, then she might perhaps have rephrased her turn of speech as an invitation. If, on the other hand, no invitation were to follow later on in the conversation, then the rules of CA say that the researcher should make no attempt to infer what B 'really' wanted to say in her turn of speech. In CA one does not speculate on the 'true' meaning of an utterance, but instead studies the means and rules by which the participants make their intentions clear and work out a common understanding. As Heritage (1984, 259) puts it: 'To summarize, conversational interaction is structured by an organization of action which is implemented on a turn-by-turn basis. By means of this organization, *a context of publicly displayed and continuously updated intersubjective understandings is systematically sustained.*'

In one sense, CA is at the heart of social theory and research, because it concentrates on analysing probably the world's oldest institution: conversations. Much of the findings of the organization of that institution have direct implications and use for an understanding of any aspects of social reality, because in one way or another all social institutions are dependent on, or variants of, ordinary conversations. On the other hand, the level at which CA moves is devoid of all particular contents of conversations. Pure conversation analysts are not even interested in the implications of their findings for society at large. In CA, speech situations and the rules people follow in those situations are not explored in order to make inferences, indirectly, about the reality outside the conversation; rather, the conversation is itself the prime object of study. As Schegloff (1992, xviii) puts it, Harvey Sacks started examining talk 'as an object in its own right, and not merely as a screen on which are projected other processes, whether Balesian system problems or Schutzian interpretive strategies, or Garfinkelian commonsense methods'.

This restriction to conversation as a reality in its own right means that the particular symbolic or rhetoric structures of meaning existing in a culture, group or era fall beyond the scope of the method. It also means that from this viewpoint, a social phenomenon can only be studied in so far as it has a 'conversational existence'. Other forms of interaction, such as that taking place via printed matter or through state officials sending announcements to citizens, are beyond its scope.

However, CA can be applied in a more or less 'orthodox' fashion in analysing qualitative research interviews or naturally occurring speech situations. As can be seen from the examples in the previous section, present-day discourse analysis has been influenced by CA. It has contributed to the 'toolbox' of contemporary qualitative analysis, where the idea of language as representation is combined in a pertinent way with the idea of language as action.

The end of interviews?

Although the recent trends in social science interviewing seem to point at increasing problems in dealing with interviews as empirical data, it would be premature to announce the end of the era of interviews. For one thing, surveys will probably continue to be part of empirical social research, even though we are better aware than before of the limits of survey analysis. Secondly, the developments in discourse and conversation analysis have made us more aware than ever before of the richness of interviews both as a source of direct or indirect knowledge about a researched topic and as a specimen of a reality in its own right.

It might seem that in the light of a discursive and constructionist approach, it is always preferable to use naturally occurring data rather than to conduct interviews. However, as Holstein and Gubrium (1995, 18) say, talk about some topics, although deeply significant, may be relatively rare in the normal course of everyday life, even in the 'interview society'. Interviews can thus be used to gain purchase on interpretive practice relating to matters that may not be casually topical. Although there are sometimes problems in relating the observations made from interview talk to other reality in a valid fashion, abstaining from interviews altogether on that basis is hardly the solution. The phenomena we deal with in social research are never easily and totally reliably at hand. In all science, we have to have the courage at some point to suggest an interpretation, even at the risk of being proven wrong.

Although social researchers will probably always continue to do interview studies, it is nevertheless useful to ask oneself whether the research design really calls for interviews. All too often in the past people have routinely done interviews, which have become equated with 'empirical data' proper, as if materials such as newspaper or magazine articles, other printed material, official documents, television programmes, recorded ordinary conversations or other naturally occurring data were somehow less 'empirical' or convincing. This is partly due to the previously prevalent and self-evident notion of empirical social research as 'behavioural science', studying individuals' behaviour and attitudes, and reducing all social phenomena to individuals and their interaction. Another incentive for conducting interviews has been the idea that through them ordinary people, minorities or oppressed groups are 'given voice'.

Neither of these two motives for interviewing is unquestionable, however. For one thing, although – and especially because – modern (and 'postmodern' or 'late modern') culture celebrates individualism and individuality, we should not uncritically adopt the view that the individual is the centre of human reality. Secondly, the discursive approach to interviews and other conversations problematizes the romantic idea of an authentic voice or true inner feelings and meanings that can be captured by an in-depth interview. To get a grasp of social phenomena, people must certainly be heard, but there is no privileged position from which 'the truth' can be received. It is always up to the researcher to argue for an interpretation, no matter what the research materials consist of.

CHAPTER 10

DETECTIVE STORIES AND SOCIOLOGICAL LITERATURE

There are many fascinating similarities between detective stories and social research as a literary genre, which I here for brevity call sociological literature. The principal attraction of both lies in the process of intellectual inference, but the structures of the two textual genres are quite different. In detective stories the author typically tells a fictional story of chronological events through which the hero or heroes solve a mystery, whereas in sociological literature the author or authors perform a long monologue in which they first present a mystery to the reader and then, after presenting the evidence and weighing it, suggest an answer.

The events and phenomena at the centre of attention are also different, yet the basic elements of human inference are the same. Both literary genres make it clear that the material collected for the case will only be transformed into interesting and relevant observations once the investigators have been able to distance themselves from self-evident presumptions within which they are normally perceived – or overlooked. In examining these observations in the light of different frameworks, the investigator is looking at the clues of the case. As soon as the pieces of the jigsaw slot into place, the investigator will submit those clues as evidence to back up the solution proposed.

Another feature that detective stories and sociological research share in common is that both are concerned with making rational inferences about meaningful activity and phenomena and events related to human relations. This probably goes some way towards explaining the similarities that are found in the history of the social sciences and detective stories.

There are also differences, of course. For instance, it is clear that detective stories have no equivalent to the various methods and theoretical approaches that we have in social research. The history of social research includes many periods which turn to the past, to methodic and theoretical solutions that are considered outmoded. For instance, the 1950s and 1960s were a golden age for statistical methods, even though they had been widely criticized by the 1930s. The field of contemporary social research includes representatives of all the above-mentioned methodic and theoretical approaches as well as individual studies that have successfully used different methods side by side.

The parallel features in the historical development of detective stories and sociological literature are mainly due to the fact that all types of literature mirror (within the confines of the means accessible to each genre) what is happening in the world around them at that particular time. Detective stories and sociological literature are no exception in this respect. The only inference to be drawn from the fact that there are so many connections at so many levels between detective stories and sociology is that these genres are closely related.

Sociology as a force of influence in society

One of the distinctive features of sociology is that it is a genre of non-fiction, a type of literature which tells us about what is happening in society or what we know about society and social phenomena. In this sense sociology, just as other categories of non-fiction, has a very special status among all the genres of literature. Sociology is often used as the provider of the facts on the basis of which other genres are located in time and in society. That is, in explaining historical developments in other genres of literature people often resort to social research as the provider of the true social context that makes those developments understandable.

However, there are many sociologists who argue that knowledge about society should be approached and considered not only from the point of view of its truth-value. Forms of knowledge and the methods and organization of knowledge acquisition are in themselves forms of power and social institutions. This observation refers not only to the fact that information concerning individuals can be used against them. Also (and this has more far-reaching implications), it must be recognized that through the concepts, models and classification criteria that are used in collecting data for administrative purposes and for social research, sociological literature contributes to constructing the whole notion of 'society' and 'social reality', and the named objects in that reality. Forms of power entail types of social organization – such as prisons, hospitals, schools, parliaments and governments – which then place individuals in particular subject positions, opening up whole fields and forms of knowledge and research. This leads into a continuous two-way process, where organizational arrangements produce forms of knowledge, and the discourses within which those organizations are talked about and reflected on lead to changes and reforms in those organizations. From this viewpoint, the formation of different disciplines within the sociological literature can be seen in connection with the development in social institutions. According to Foucault (1979, 224), the development of modern human sciences was particularly accelerated in the eighteenth century:

At this point, the disciplines crossed the 'technological' threshold. First the hospital, then the school, then, later, the workshop were not simply reordered by the disciplines; they became, thanks to them, apparatuses such that any mechanism of objectification could be used in them as an instrument of subjection, and any growth of power could give rise in them to possible branches of knowledge; it was this link, proper to the technological systems, that made possible within the disciplinary element the formation of clinical medicine, psychiatry, child psychology, educational psychology, the rationalization of labour. It is a double process, then: an epistemological 'thaw' through a refinement of power relations; a multiplication of the effects of power through the formation and accumulation of new forms of knowledge.

In other words, as a form of literature, social research not only produces impartial accounts of social reality. Like it or not, through their research and accounts social researchers contribute to changing the very reality that they seem to analyse in the first place. We could say that research has created and continues to create society in its own image.

We must not, however, overestimate sociological literature in its ability to produce systems of categorizing reality that are then used by readers of literature as a basis for their subjective intellectual, aesthetic and emotional experiences. It would be arrogant to argue that 'in the beginning was the Word': that social research is in the position of God. There is no reason to set sociological literature apart from other genres of literature, because it is far from being the only type of writing that affects our images of social reality and the measures taken on the basis of those images. Its position in society depends first and foremost on the historical moment. Lepenies (1988) says that ever since the mid-nineteenth century there has been an ongoing battle in France, Britain and later in Germany between sociology and (fictional) literature as to which of the two provides the primary model of orientation to modern civilization, or the primary model for living in industrial society. We must also bear in mind that public discussion in contemporary society is permeated by different, competing notions of social reality and accounts of social conditions. Although politicians may refer to social research in their arguments, that is often done in a purposeful fashion, to legitimize a political decision already made. Inquiries may be commissioned by government offices precisely to provide justification for such decisions.

Social research can influence society and social development in two main ways. What is often termed 'humanist' research has first of all affected the formation of national identity, whereas 'empirical social research' has primarily produced knowledge about society and its population groups used in political decision-making. The former type of research is directed to the large reading public, whereas the latter 'social technological' research does not necessarily need publicity in order to have an impact.

Much of social research contains elements from both these orientations. Academic research at least is public and has some influence on public opinion. On the other hand, there is also much research which is concerned to demonstrate, by reference to its empirical results, the actual state of affairs in reality.

It seems that the 1980s and 1990s have witnessed a slight shift in the primary target group of sociological literature towards the general public. The increasing popularity of cultural studies and the constructionist approach can in that sense be seen as a partial merger of 'humanist' and 'social' research. From this viewpoint social research is seen as an exercise of analysing, deconstructing and breaking old and established ways of thinking about society and the way it works. This shift has also been described as a crisis of the authority of expert systems (Beck et al. 1994), and linked with the collapse of state socialism and centralized systems of social planning in capitalist societies. Well aware of the risks involved in the elitist role of ideologue, sociologists are increasingly cautious about submitting alternative positive models.

However, the production of data describing social reality and intended for purposes of political decision-making has by no means lost its significance; witness the numerous studies by feminist scholars on the role and status of women in society. Cultural critique and the production of new information are not in conflict with one another. The new information produced in women's studies, for instance, comes from an analysis of empirical material which is based on new frames of references and new classification criteria. Rantalaiho (1988) says that there are two methodological approaches in women's studies. On the one hand, there is the line of work which lays bare, which transforms the invisible into the visible. On the other hand, there is the deconstructive line which critically examines the deep-seated ways of thinking and established divisions that structure everyday life and the studies of normal science.

Sociology as a genre of literature

It is not difficult to argue and defend the view that sociology is a form of literature. For instance, you could point out that the end-product of sociology is always in the form of a written report. However, the analogy as such is a waste of time if there is no substance to it, if it doesn't offer anything specific and concrete. Surely it makes more sense to talk about social research or sociology as a *discipline*? The difference between literature and science, of course, is that while literature is in the business of providing entertainment and adventures, science is about producing hard facts on the basis of objective observations and logical conclusions. Surely the outcomes of social research should be objective and logically sound.

The two views of sociology as either a scientific discipline or literature highlight different aspects of sociology and point at different sides of its role in society. For instance, empirical social research would define itself as a discipline whose results have an influence on political decision-making. This is reflected in the terminology that is used in social research. The products of its work are often called *research reports*, not studies or sociological literature. The research process is distinguished from the end-product because doing research consists of much more than just writing up the research report: designing the problem, reading up on earlier research and research results, choosing appropriate methods, collecting and analysing data.

As for the view that social research is a genre of literature, the point here is that the text is all the audience ever sees of social research; this is the only proof that it exists. The accent is on the role that research plays in undoing old established ways of thinking. This cultural critique approach requires a careful weighing of language and style issues. Firstly, the requirement of publicity means that the results of research must be presented in a readily digestible and, importantly, interesting way. Secondly, the critique of old images and associations means that researchers have to pay special attention not only to logical coherence and clarity, but also to representation and to the figures of speech they use.

Writing up research is essentially a process of working with words; and words, with all their meanings and shades of meaning, are an integral part of our cultural heritage. The language we use relies in large part on the use of metaphors or *tropes*. In trying to explain what we mean when we are talking about, say, society or culture, we are never able exactly to say what we mean, nor do we mean exactly what we say. When we want to describe something or to make a more refined point, we have to use comparisons and metaphors, and content ourselves with the tropes that are in common usage. Scientific reporting is expected to avoid the pitfalls of tropes, but Hayden White (1978) says that this requirement is doomed to failure: it is precisely through these tropes that a publication constitutes the objects that it pretends to describe realistically and to analyse objectively. For instance, White's (ibid., 16–17) studies of the styles and metaphors used by historians and social scientists include an analysis of E.P. Thompson's *The Making of the English Working Class* (1963). Thompson begins his work with an attack on earlier researchers who have taken for granted the laws that determine the formation of social classes: instead of abstract theorizing, he defends his own approach, which studies the history of the working class in concrete terms. But no sooner has Thompson pilloried Smelser and Dahrendorf than Thompson himself says: 'This book can be seen as a biography of the English working class from its adolescence until its early manhood' (ibid., 11), as if such culturally determined metaphors were any less problematical.

If sociology is reduced to a genre of literature, and if it is impossible to represent objective truths, then why bother to collect empirical data to prove the validity of one's results and conclusions? Why should sociology be based on logical argumentation in the first place?

This is precisely what makes the genre of sociological literature. There is nothing to stop us from throwing these premises of sociological literature overboard and starting from scratch – but the outcome would not necessarily be regarded as sociological literature. An example of different genres is provided by pamphlets on social issues, which had an important role to play in the 1960s in making known the views and demands of various single-issue movements. However, sociological literature is a special case in the sense that publications considered to represent this particular genre are accepted as academic dissertations. The boundaries of sociology are by no means watertight, and they change with time. Owing to its special academic status, it is indeed useful every now and then to check whether the existing boundaries are really relevant, to see what is regarded as sociological research and what is not. Most recently, the growth of cultural studies and women's studies has made it necessary to revise the lines of demarcation.

However, not everything that is distinctive of sociology is an indication of the profession's narrow-mindedness. Sociology is literature which promotes rational debate about important issues in society. At its best, sociology can open up fresh and relevant perspectives on those issues and help reach a deeper understanding of what is happening in society. It can help to uncover the structures and underlying contingencies of different compulsions and inevitabilities and in so doing help the reader find new avenues for action. All this requires a capacity for logical conclusions and a measure of creativeness, but also the right kind of tools to help achieve success. It is from this point of view that we should examine theories, the use of empirical data and related methodic rules. If the concepts and methods are intended simply to give an academic ring to the text, they will be of no avail. A theoretical framework is a way of thinking about something, a way of thematizing and perceiving a certain phenomenon that is different from the everyday perception; the method is the way in which that framework is applied to the subject of the study. The method has a dual role. On the one hand, material that is organized according to the rules of the method will tell the researcher what conclusions may be drawn from that material. The method provides protection against being carried away by one's own presumptions. On the other hand, the method is like a telescope or a microscope which sheds light on the object of study in a new, fresh way. It can raise issues that might not be visible to the naked eye; things that might give clues of yet another framework.

The same obviously applies to the empirical material, because the empirical data are represented in the study by any material which is organized according to the rules of the method. The empirical material also has a dual role. On the one hand, it provides direct or indirect information on the matter or phenomenon in question. On the other hand, the empirical material (whether it consists of observations or interviews, a sample of cultural products or a collection of reports by other social scientists) is 'food for thought': material against which researchers can sharpen their conceptual and methodic tools.

But sociology cannot be reduced to innovative methods of data collection or to clever inferences; at the end of the day it is about researchers' way of commenting on the world, presenting their own interpretation of what is going on. Theoretical perspectives and methodic innovations are entirely useless if the subject and message of the study are not meaningful and important to readers and indeed to researchers themselves. Although sociologists must always remain critical towards their own preconceptions, they do need to have a vision of society, its past, the utopias and threats on the future horizon. It is only on this basis that the themes and research interests will grow up which will steer them towards theoretical frameworks and methodic solutions.

REFERENCES

Alasuutari, Pertti (1986) Alcoholism in Its Cultural Context: The Case of Blue-collar Men. *Contemporary Drug Problems* 13, 641–686.

Alasuutari, Pertti (1992) *Desire and Craving: A Cultural Theory of Alcoholism.* New York: State University of New York Press.

Alasuutari, Pertti (1995) *Researching Culture: Qualitative Method and Cultural Studies.* London: Sage.

Alasuutari, Pertti (ed.) (forthcoming) *The Inscribed Audience: The New Agenda of Media Reception and Audience Ethnography.* London: Sage.

Alasuutari, Pertti and Juha Kytömäki (1986) Pahuus on tappava bumerangi: *Vanha kettu-televisiosarjan maailmankuva ja juonirakenne* [Badness is a Deadly Boomerang: The World View and Narrative Structure of the Television Series *Der Alte*]. In Kalle Heikkinen (ed.), *Kymmenen esseetä elämäntavasta* [Ten Essays on the Way of Life]. Lahti: Oy Yleisradio Ab, 139–152.

Allor, Martin (1988) Relocating the Site of the Audience. *Critical Studies in Mass Communication* 5, 217–233.

Ang, Ien (1985) *Watching Dallas: Soap Opera and the Melodramatic Imagination.* London: Methuen.

Ang, Ien (1991) *Desperately Seeking the Audience.* London: Routledge.

Asplund, Johan (1978) *Bertillon og Holmes.* Copenhagen: Forlaget Klods-Hans.

Atkinson, J. Maxwell and Paul Drew (1979) *Order in Court: The Organization of Verbal Interaction in Judicial Settings.* London: Macmillan.

Austin, J.L. (1962) *How to do Things with Words.* London: Oxford University Press.

Beck, Ulrich, Anthony Giddens and Scott Lash (1994) *Reflexive Modernization: Politics, Tradition and Aesthetics in the Modern Social Order.* Stanford, CA: Stanford University Press.

Benjamin, Walter (1973) *Charles Baudelaire: A Lyric Poet in the Era of High Capitalism.* London: New Left Books.

Berg, Bruce L. (1989) *Qualitative Research Methods for the Social Sciences.* Boston: Allyn & Bacon.

Bernal, J.D. (1971) *Science in History, Volume 4: The Social Sciences: Conclusion.* Cambridge, MA: MIT Press.

Bernard, H. Russell (1988) *Research Methods in Cultural Anthropology.* Newbury Park, CA: Sage.

Blumer, Herbert (1986) *Symbolic Interactionism: Perspective and Method.* Berkeley, CA: University of California Press.

Bogdan, Robert and Steven J. Taylor (1975) *Introduction to Qualitative Research Methods: A Phenomenological Approach to the Social Sciences.* New York: John Wiley & Sons.

Bourdieu, Pierre (1984) *Distinction: A Social Critique of the Judgement of Taste.* Cambridge, MA: Harvard University Press.

Clarke, John, Chas Critcher and Richard Johnson (eds) (1979) *Working Class Culture.* London: Hutchinson.

Clifford, James and George E. Marcus (1986) *Writing Culture: The Poetics and Politics of Ethnography.* Berkeley: University of California Press.

Derrida, Jacques (1976) *Of Grammatology.* Baltimore: Johns Hopkins University Press.

Dooley, David (1990) *Social Research Methods.* Second edition. Englewood Cliffs, NJ: Prentice Hall.

Durkheim, Émile (1954) *The Elementary Forms of the Religious Life.* London: Allen & Unwin.

Durkheim, Émile (1966) *Suicide: A Study in Sociology.* New York: Free Press.

Eco, Umberto (1976) *A Theory of Semiotics.* Bloomington: Indiana University Press.

Eco, Umberto and Thomas A. Sebeok (eds) (1983) *The Sign of Three: Dupin, Holmes, Peirce.* Bloomington: Indiana University Press.

Elias, Norbert (1978) *The History of Manners. The Civilizing Process, Volume I.* New York: Pantheon Books.

Elias, Norbert (1982) *Power and Civility. The Civilizing Process, Volume II.* New York: Pantheon Books.

Engels, Friedrich (1987) *The Condition of the Working Class in England.* Harmondsworth: Penguin.

Eskola, Antti (1971) *Sosiologian tutkimusmenetelmät II (Sociological Research Methods II).* Porvoo: WSOY.

Eskola, Antti (1988) *Blind Alleys in Social Psychology: A Search for Ways Out.* Amsterdam: North-Holland.

Falk, Pasi and Pekka Sulkunen (1983) Drinking on the Screen: An Analysis of a Mythical Male Fantasy in Finnish Films. *Social Science Information* 22 (3), 387–410.

Fink, Arlene (1995) *How to Ask Survey Questions.* Thousand Oaks, CA: Sage.

Foucault, Michel (1978) *The History of Sexuality, Volume I: An Introduction.* New York: Vintage Books.

Foucault, Michel (1979) *Discipline and Punish: The Birth of the Prison.* New York: Vintage Books.

Garbarino, Merwyn S. (1983) *Sociocultural Theory in Anthropology: A Short History.* Prospect Heights, IL: Waveland Press.

Garfinkel, Harold (1984) *Studies in Ethnomethodology.* Cambridge: Polity Press.

Geertz, Clifford (1973) *The Interpretation of Cultures.* New York: Basic Books.

Geertz, Clifford (1988) *Works and Lives: The Anthropologist as Author.* Cambridge: Polity Press.

Georges, Robert A. and Michael O. Jones (1980) *People Studying People: The Human Element in Fieldwork.* Berkeley: University of California Press.

Ginzburg, Carlo (1983) Morelli, Freud, and Sherlock Holmes: Clues and Scientific Method. In Umberto Eco and Thomas A. Sebeok (eds), *The Sign of Three: Dupin, Holmes, Peirce.* Bloomington: Indiana University Press, 81–118.

Goffman, Erving (1974) *Frame Analysis: An Essay on the Organization of Experience.* Cambridge, MA: Harvard University Press.

Goldfrank, Walter L. (1972) Reappraising Le Play. In Anthony Oberschall (ed.), *The Establishment of Empirical Sociology: Studies in Continuity, Discontinuity and Institutionalization.* New York: Harper & Row, 130–151.

Grossberg, Lawrence (1988) Wandering Audiences, Nomadic Critics. *Cultural Studies* 2 (3), 377–392.

Gupta, Akhil and James Ferguson (1997) Discipline and Practice: 'The Field' as Site, Method, and Location in Anthropology. In Akhil Gupta and James Ferguson, *Anthropological Locations: Boundaries and Grounds of a Field Science.* Berkeley: University of California Press, 1–46.

Hall, Stuart and Tony Jefferson (eds) (1975) *Resistance Through Rituals: Youth Subcultures in Post-war Britain.* London: Hutchinson.

Harré, Rom and P.F. Secord (1972) *The Explanation of Social Behaviour.* Oxford: Basil Blackwell.

Hart, Elizabeth and Meg Bond (1995) *Action Research for Health and Social Care: A Guide to Practice.* Buckingham: Open University Press.

Hebdige, Dick (1979) *Subculture: The Meaning of Style.* London: Methuen.

Heritage, John (1984) *Garfinkel and Ethnomethodology.* Cambridge: Polity Press.

Hoggart, Richard (1957) *The Uses of Literacy.* Harmondsworth: Penguin.

Holstein, James A. and Jaber F. Gubrium (1995) *The Active Interview.* Qualitative Research Methods Series 37. Thousand Oaks, CA: Sage.

Inkeles, Alex (1969) Making Men Modern: On the Causes and Consequences of Individual Change in Six Developing Countries. *American Journal of Sociology* 35 (2), 208–225.

Jay, Martin (1974) *The Dialectical Imagination: A History of the Frankfurt School and the Institute of Social Research 1923–50.* London: Heinemann.

Jones, Gareth Stedman (1983) *Languages of Class: Studies in English Working Class History 1832–1982.* Cambridge: Cambridge University Press.

Kent, Raymond (1981) *A History of British Empirical Sociology.* Farnborough: Gower.

Koski-Jännes, Anja (1992) *Alcohol Addiction and Self-regulation: A Controlled Trial of a Relapse Prevention Program for Finnish Inpatient Alcoholics.* Helsinki: The Finnish Foundation for Alcohol Studies, Volume 41.

Kvale, Steinar (1996) *Interviews: An Introduction to Qualitative Research Interviewing.* Thousand Oaks, CA: Sage.

Laclau, Ernesto (1983) Transformations of Advanced Industrial Societies and the Theory of the Subject. In Sakari Hänninen and Leena Paldan (eds), *Rethinking Ideology: A Marxist Debate*. Argument Sonderband AS 84. Berlin: Argument-Verlag, 39–44.

Lazarsfeld, Paul F. (1961) Notes on the History of Quantification in Sociology — Trends, Sources and Problems. *Isis* 52 (2), 277–333.

Lazarsfeld, Paul F. (1968) Foreword. In Morris Rosenberg, *The Logic of Survey Analysis*. New York: Basic Books, vii–x.

Lefebvre, Henri (1971) *Everyday Life in the Modern World*. London: Allen Lane/Penguin.

Lejeune, Philippe (1989) *On Autobiography*. Minneapolis: University of Minnesota Press.

Lepenies, Wolf (1988) *Between Literature and Science: The Rise of Sociology*. Cambridge: Cambridge University Press.

Lévi-Strauss, Claude (1968) *Structural Anthropology*. London: Allen Lane/Penguin.

McNiff, Jean (1994) *Action Research: Principles and Practice*. London: Routledge.

Malinowski, Bronislaw (1961) *Argonauts of the Western Pacific*. New York: E.P. Dutton.

Mannheim, Karl (1979) *Ideology and Utopia: An Introduction to the Sociology of Knowledge*. London: Lund Humphries.

Maranda, Pierre and Elli Köngäs Maranda (1971) *Structural Analysis of Oral Tradition*. Philadelphia: University of Pennsylvania Press.

Marcus, George E. and Michael M.J. Fischer (1986) *Anthropology as Cultural Critique: An Experimental Moment in the Human Sciences*. Chicago: University of Chicago Press.

Marsh, Peter, Elizabeth Rosser and Rom Harré (1978) *The Rules of Disorder*. London: Routledge & Kegan Paul.

Marx, Karl (1976) Theses on Feuerbach. In Karl Marx and Frederick Engels, *Collected Works, Volume 5*. Moscow: Progress Publishers, 1–5.

Marx, Karl (1977) *Capital, Volume I*. New York: Random House.

Mead, George Herbert (1962) *Mind, Self, and Society*. Chicago: University of Chicago Press.

Mills, C. Wright (1977) *The Sociological Imagination*. New York: Penguin Books.

Mungham, G. and Geoffrey Pearson (1976) *Working Class Youth Culture*. London: Routledge & Kegan Paul.

Nofsinger, Robert E. (1991) *Everyday Conversation*. Newbury Park, CA: Sage.

Oberschall, Anthony (1965) *Empirical Social Research in Germany*. Paris: Mouton.

Park, Robert E., Ernest W. Burgess and Roderick D. McKenzie (1967) *The City*. Chicago: University of Chicago Press.

Petty, Sir William (1963) *Political Arithmetick*. In Charles Henry Hull (ed.), *The Economic Writings of Sir William Petty, Volume I*. New York: Reprints of Economic Classics, Augustus M. Kelley, Bookseller, 232–313.

Potter, Jonathan (1996) *Representing Reality: Discourse, Rhetoric and Social Construction*. London: Sage.

Potter, Jonathan and Margaret Wetherell (1987) *Discourse and Social Psychology: Beyond Attitudes and Behaviour*. London: Sage.

Propp, Vladimir (1975) *Morphology of the Folktale*. Austin and London: University of Texas Press.

Rabinow, Paul (1977) *Reflections on Fieldwork in Morocco*. Berkeley: University of California Press.

Radway, Janice A. (1984) *Reading the Romance: Women, Patriarchy, and Popular Literature*. Chapel Hill: University of North Carolina Press.

Radway, Janice (1988) Reception Study: Ethnography and the Problems of Dispersed Audiences and Nomadic Subjects. *Cultural Studies* 2 (3), 359–376.

Ragin, Charles C. (1994) *Constructing Social Research: The Unity and Diversity of Method*. Thousand Oaks, CA: Pine Forge Press.

Rantalaiho, Liisa (1988) Naistutkimuksen metodologiasta [On the Methodology of Women's Studies]. In Päivi Setälä and Hannele Kurki (eds), *Akanvirtaan*. Helsinki: Yliopistopaino, 28–54.

Reason, Peter and John Rowan (eds) (1981) *Human Inquiry: A Sourcebook of New Paradigm Research*. Chichester: John Wiley.

Rigby, Peter (1977) Critical Participation, Mere Observation or Alienation? *Development and Culture Research, Jipemoyo I, No. I*, Helsinki.

Rorty, Richard (1982) *Consequences of Pragmatism: Essays 1972–1980*. Minneapolis: University of Minnesota Press.

Rosenberg, Morris (1968) *The Logic of Survey Analysis*. New York: Basic Books.

Rosenzweig, Roy (1983) *Eight Hours for What We Will: Workers and Leisure in an Industrial City, 1870–1920*. Cambridge: Cambridge University Press.

Rumelhart, David E. (1977) Understanding and Summarizing Brief Stories. In David Laberge and S. Jay Samuels (eds), *Basic Processes in Reading: Perception and Comprehension*. Hillsdale, NJ: Lawrence Erlbaum Associates, 265–303.

Saussure, Ferdinand de (1966) *Course in General Linguistics*. New York: McGraw-Hill.

Schegloff, Emanuel A. (1992) Introduction. In Harvey Sacks, *Lectures on Conversation, Volume I*. Oxford: Blackwell, ix–lxii.

Searle, John R. (1976) The Classification of Illocutionary Acts. *Language in Society* 5, 1–24.

Sebeok, Thomas A. and Jean Umiker-Sebeok (1983) 'You Know My Method': A Juxtaposition of Charles S. Peirce and Sherlock Holmes. In Umberto Eco and Thomas A. Sebeok (eds), *The Sign of Three: Dupin, Holmes, Peirce*. Bloomington: Indiana University Press, 11–54.

Selvin, Hannan C. (1985) Durkheim, Booth and Yule: The Non-Diffusion of an Intellectual Innovation. In Martin Bulmer (ed.), *Essays on the History of British Sociological Research*. Cambridge: Cambridge University Press, 70–82.

Shalvey, Thomas (1979) *Claude Lévi-Strauss: Social Psychotherapy and the Collective Unconscious*. Amherst, MA: University of Massachusetts Press.

Stewart, John O. (1989) *Drinkers, Drummers, and Decent Folk: Ethnographic Narratives of Village Trinidad*. New York: State University of New York Press.

Sutcliffe, Claud R. (1978) Education as a Dependent Variable in the Process of Modernization. *Journal of Social Psychology* 104, 3–7.

Swantz, Marja-Liisa and Deborah Bryceson (1976) *Women Workers in Dar es Salaam*. Dar es Salaam: Bureau of Research Assessment and Land Use Planning.

Symons, Julian (1992) *Bloody Murder: From the Detective Story to the Crime Novel: A History*. London: Pan Books.

Tannen, Deborah (1993) What's in a Frame? Surface Evidence for Underlying Expectations. In Deborah Tannen (ed.), *Framing in Discourse*. New York: Oxford University Press, 14–56.

Thompson, E.P. (1963) *The Making of the English Working Class*. New York: Vintage Books.

Thrasher, Frederick M. (1960) *The Gang: A Study of 1,313 Gangs in Chicago*. Chicago: University of Chicago Press.

Touraine, Alain (1981) *The Voice and the Eye*. Cambridge: Cambridge University Press.

Trilling, Lionel (1971) *Sincerity and Authenticity*. Cambridge, MA: Harvard University Press.

Vilkko, Anni (1988) Eletty elämä, kerrottu elämä, tarinoitunut elämä – omaelämäkerta ja yhteisymmärrrys [Biography and Mutual Understanding]. *Sosiologia* 25, 81–90.

Weber, Max (1978) *Economy and Society. An Outline of Interpretative Sociology, Volume One*. Berkeley: University of California Press.

White, Hayden (1978) *Tropics of Discourse: Essays in Cultural Criticism*. Baltimore: Johns Hopkins University Press.

Whorf, Benjamin Lee (1956) *Language, Thought, and Reality: Selected Writings of Benjamin Lee Whorf*. Cambridge, MA: MIT Press.

Whyte, William Foote (1981) *Street Corner Society: The Social Structure of an Italian Slum*. Chicago: University of Chicago Press.

Whyte, William Foote (1984) *Learning from the Field: A Guide from Experience*. Beverly Hills, CA: Sage.

Widdicombe, Sue and Robin Wooffitt (1995) *The Language of Youth Subcultures: Social Identity in Action*. Hemel Hempstead: Harvester Wheatsheaf.

Williams, Raymond (1982) *Culture and Society 1780–1950*. Harmondsworth: Penguin.

Williams, Raymond (1988) *Keywords: A Vocabulary of Culture and Society*. London: Fontana Press.

Willis, Paul (1974) Symbolism and Practice: A Theory for the Social Meaning of Pop Music. *Centre for Contemporary Cultural Studies, Stencilled Paper* No. 13.

Willis, Paul (1977) *Learning to Labour. How Working Class Kids Get Working Class Jobs*. Farnborough: Gower.

Willis, Paul (1978) *Profane Culture*. London: Routledge & Kegan Paul.

Wright, Will (1977) *Sixguns and Society: A Structural Study of the Western*. Berkeley and Los Angeles: University of California Press.

Yates, Frances (1969) Bacon and the Menace of English Lit. *New York Review of Books*, 27 March, 37.

INDEX

abstracted empiricism, 87, 88
abstraction
  in quantifying method, 40
    Marx's work, 41–3
    surveys, 50, 53
action research, 88–92, 134
active interviewing, 148–9
administrative apparatus, 11–15
Adventures of Caleb Williams, The, 3
Adventures of Sherlock Holmes, The,
  1
  see also Holmes
Ang, Ien, 128
anthropology
  crisis of representation, 75, 76–7
  features of, 59–61
  Malinowski's work, 61–3
  structuralist, 99
Argonauts of the Western Pacific, 61
Asplund, Johan, 3, 22
attitude measurement, 49
audiences
  discursive approach to, 128
  interpretation of stories, 125–6
  reception of stories, 122–4

Balzac, Honoré de, 14
behavioural psychology, 22
Benjamin, Walter, 18, 20, 21
Bentham, Jeremy, 13, 16
Bertillon, Alphonse, 15, 22

Birmingham Centre for
  Contemporary Cultural
  Studies, 74–5, 109
Black Mask tradition, 81–3
Blue Hammer, 82
Blumer, Herbert, 101
Bourdieu, Pierre, 55–7, 108

CA (conversation analysis), 152–4
*Capital: A Critique of Political
  Economy*, 1, 41–4
capitalism
  Marx's work on, 41–4
  social research on, 17
causal relationships, and surveys,
  53–5
Chandler, Raymond, 28, 33, 87, 88
Chicago School, 73–4
Christie, Agatha, 29–30, 31
class
  Bourdieu's study of, 108
  studies of working class, 72–3,
    106–7, 109–10
clients, in crime novels, 83
clues
  and evidence, 32, 33–4
  and observations, 27
collective conscious, 122
colonialism, and ethnography, 60
Conan Doyle, Sir Arthur, 1–2, 4, 6,
  132
  see also Holmes

control groups, 46, 47, 48
conversation
  in detective stories, 131–4
  see also interviews
conversation analysis (CA), 152–4
crime novels
  genre of, 81–4
  see also detective stories
criminal technology, 15, 22
critical theory, 84–8
cultural capital, 56
cultural products
  discursive analysis of, 127–8
  paradigmatic analysis of, 116–18
  reception of stories, 122–4
  schema theory of interpretation,
    125–6, 127
  study of, 115–16, 128–9
  syntagmatic analysis of, 118–20
  Wright's analysis of, 120–2
cultural studies, 115–16

Davenant, Charles, 12
deconstructionism, 113
deduction
  in detective stories and social
    research, 35
  in nineteenth century, 19–22
  role of observation, 27
  and solution, 31–2
dependent variables
  in experimental design, 46, 47–8
  in surveys, 53, 54
Der Alte, 123–4
Derrida, Jacques, 113
detective stories
  audience reception of *Der Alte*,
    123–4
  Black Mask tradition, 81–3
  compared with social research,
    6–7, 34–5, 157–8
  as exercise in logic, 6–7
  growth of, 20, 21–2
  link with psychology, 22
  models of explanation in, 31–2
  research methods in, 28–31
  role of dialogue in, 131–4
  social context of, 1, 4–5
  and social order debate, 2–3

theoretical frameworks in, 30
turn to crime novels, 81–4
detectives, in crime novels, 82–3
dialogue
  in detective stories, 131–4
  see also conversation analysis;
    interviews
differences
  ethnographic research on, 59–60,
    61, 68
  quantification of, 58
disciplines
  formation of, 159
  sociology as, 162
discourse analysis, 127–8, 135
discursive interviews, 145–51
Domesday Book, 11, 12
drunkenness, paradigmatic
  analysis of, 117–18
Durkheim, Émile, 44–5, 47–8, 55,
    103–5

economy
  dimensions of, 17
  impact on social research, 17–19
  Marx's work on capitalism, 41–4
educational capital, 56
*Elementary Forms of the Religious
    Life, The*, 103–5
Elias, Norbert, 10
empirical research
  emergence of, 9–12
  impact of exchange economy
    on, 17–19
  influence of, 160–1
  nineteenth century expansion of,
    19
  role of, 164
Engels, Friedrich, 72–3
*Enquiry Concerning the Principles of
    Political Justice*, 3
ethics
  of ethnography, 78
  of experimental design, 47
  of survey research, 52
ethnographic research
  compared with quantitative
    research, 60
  crisis of representation in, 75–7

ethics of, 78
features of, 61, 63–5
observant participation, 66–71
origins of, 59, 60, 72
participant observation, 61–6
presumptions of, 78–80
role of theory in, 65–6, 70–1
studies of romance readership, 122–3
studies of working class, 72–3
studies of youth cultures, 70, 73–5
study of commonalities, 68, 78–80
study of difference, 59–60, 61, 68
validity in, 62–3
ethnomethodology, 67, 79–80
see also conversation analysis
ethogenic approach, 30, 142–4
evidence, and clues, 32, 33–4
exchange economy *see* economy
experimental design, 46–8
experimental groups, 46, 47, 48
explanatory models
deduction and solution in, 31–2
presented in social science, 34–5

factist perspective, 132
Falk, Pasi, 117–18
Farewell My Lovely, 33
films, Wright's analysis of Westerns, 120–2
folk tales, syntagmatic analysis of, 118–20
Foucault, Michel, 16, 92–4, 159
frames, 127
Frankfurt School, 84–6
Freud, Sigmund, 4

generalizability, 36, 49, 79
Ginzburg, Carlo, 3–4
Godwin, William, 3
Goffman, Erving, 127
Graunt, John, 11–12
Grossberg, Lawrence, 77
Gubrium, Jaber F., 148–9, 155

habitus, 108

Hammett, Dashiell, 81–2, 84, 134
Harré, Rom, 142
Hercule Poirot's Christmas, 29–30
Heritage, John, 153
Hoggart, Richard, 74
Holmes, Sherlock
clues and evidence, 33–4
context of stories, 1–2
methods of, 3–4, 27, 29, 31–2, 132
and observation, 26, 27, 65–6
popularity of, 21
theoretical framework of, 30
Holstein, James A., 148–9, 155
homology, 108–11
Horkheimer, Max, 86
Hound of the Baskervilles, The, 30
House in Turk Street, The, 134
human engineering, 90–1
humanist research, influence of, 160–1

Ideology and Utopia, 85–6
in-depth interviews, 141–5
independent variables
in experimental design, 46, 48
in surveys, 53, 54
individual, emerging concept of, 11
inference
in detective stories and social research, 34
role of observation, 27
see also deduction
informants
approaches to, 135–6
perceptions of surveys, 140–1
rapport with, 144–5
Inkeles, Alex, 54
interaction perspective, 133–4
interpretive repertoires, 127
interpretive sociology, 79
interviews
active interviewing, 148–9
continued use of, 154–6
discursive, 145–51
as form of interaction, 136–9

interviews, *cont.*
  importance in detective stories,
    132, 133–4
  importance in social research,
    131
  in-depth, 141–5
  nature of survey interviews,
    135–41
  in quantifying method, 49, 51–2
  of romance readers, 122
  validity of, 139–41, 144–5

knowledge
  accumulated in social science,
    35–6
  and power, 16, 159
Kvale, Steinar, 144, 145

Lady in the Lake, The, 28
language
  Saussure's theory of, 99–102
  see also semiotics
Le Play, Frédéric, 19
Lefebvre, Henri, 98–9
Lepenies, Wolf, 160
Lévi-Strauss, Claude, 99, 112, 113,
    116–17
Lewin, Kurt, 88
life-stories, 126–7
literature
  sociology as genre of, 161–5
  see also stories

MacDonald, Ross, 82, 133
McNiff, Jean, 90
Maigret, Superintendent, 31
*Making of the English Working
  Class, The*, 163
Malinowski, Bronislaw, 61–7
Mannheim, Karl, 85–6
Marlowe, Philip, 28, 33, 87, 88
Marple, Miss, 29
Marsh, Peter, 143
Marx, Karl, 1, 41–4, 90
Marxism, and critical theory, 85–6
Mayhew, Henry, 72–3
Mead, George Herbert, 99
media *see* films; stories; television
media studies, 77, 128

methodology, focus on, 6
methods *see* research methods
Mills, C. Wright, 86–8
monetary exchange economy *see*
    economy
Morelli, Giovanni, 4
morphological analysis, 120–2
myths, analysis of, 116–17

narrative structure
  concept of, 116
  morphological analysis, 120–2
  paradigmatic trend, 116–18
  and reception of stories, 122–4
  schema theory of interpretation,
    125–6, 127
  syntagmatic trend, 118–20
*Natural and Political Observations
  Made Upon the Bills of
  Mortality*, 11

observant participation, 66–71
observations
  and clues, 27
  participant observation, 61–6
  and presumptions, 25–6
  and survey method, 52, 53
  theoretical framework for, 28, 30
official statistics, 11–12

Panopticon, 13, 16
paradigmatic analysis, 116–18
participation
  observant participation, 66–71
  participant observation, 61–6
Peirce, Charles S., 25–6, 97, 99
Petty, William, 12, 17–18, 40
physiologies, 20–1
placebo effect, 47
Pocket Full of Rye, A, 31
Poe, Edgar Allan, 21
Poirot, Hercule, 29–30
police, in crime novels, 81–2, 83
political arithmetic, 12, 17–18
Political Arithmetick, 18
political economy, 17–18, 41
Polo, Marco, 59
post-structuralism, 113–14, 129
Potter, Jonathan, 127, 149

power, and knowledge, 16, 159
power relations
  in crime novels, 83, 88
  in social research, 87–8
presumptions, and observations,
    25–6
Propp, Vladimir, 118–20
psychology, 22

qualitative research
  conversation analysis (CA),
    152–4
  discursive interviews, 145–51
  explanatory models in, 35
  in-depth interviews, 141–5
  see also ethnographic research
quantifying method
  Durkheim's work, 44–5, 47–8, 55
  experimental design, 46–8
  explaining differences, 58
  Marx's work, 41–4
  nature of, 39–40
  surveys, 49–52, 53–7
quantitative research
  compared with ethnography, 60
  explanatory models in, 35
  panopticism in, 16
  see also statistical research
questionnaires
  approaches of, 136
  as form of interaction, 136–9
  formulation of, 50–1
Quételet, Adolphe, 19

Rabinow, Paul, 68–9
Radway, Janice, 122–3, 128
Rantalaiho, Liisa, 161
rapport, in interviews, 144–5
rational deduction, in nineteenth
    century, 19–22
Reading the Romance, 122
reality
  accessed in interviews, 145, 146,
    156
  see also social reality
Red Harvest, 81–2
relationism, Mannheim's theory
  of, 86

reliability, of survey data, 138
research methods
  role of, 164
  and theoretical frameworks,
    28–31, 37–8, 129–30
  see also ethnographic research;
    qualitative research;
    quantifying method;
    quantitative research
respondents
  approaches to, 135–6
  perceptions of surveys, 140–1
  rapport with, 144–5
romance novels, 122–3, 128
Rosenberg, Morris, 53
Rosenzweig, Roy, 106

sampling, 49–50
Sapir-Whorf hypothesis, 102
Saussure, Ferdinand de, 99–102
schema theory, 125–6, 127
Secord, P.F., 142
semiotics, 97–8
  influences on, 99–102
sexuality, history of, 92–4
Simenon, Georges, 31
Sixguns and Society, 120
slums, ethnographic research on,
    72–3
social action, Weber's theory of, 79
social movements, 89–90, 91–2
social order
  detective stories and debate on,
    2–3
  impact of surveillance on, 13–15
social reality
  accessed by interviews, 145, 146,
    156
  and cultural studies, 115–16
  influence of social research on,
    159–60
  and physical reality, 102–5
  semiotic theories of, 99–102
  study of, 97–8
social research
  accumulation of knowledge,
    35–6
  action research, 88–92, 134

social research, *cont.*
  compared with detective stories,
    6–7, 34–5, 157–8
  context of, 5, 16–17, 94–5
  critical theory of, 84–8
  criticism and reflection in, 37, 81
  emergence of, 1, 9–12
  explanatory models in, 34–5
  Foucault's approach to, 92–4
  impact of economy on, 17–19
  methods and theory in, 28–31,
    37–8, 129–30
  move to micro-analysis, 128–9
  nineteenth century growth of, 19
  process of deduction in, 34–5
  role of conversation in, 131–2
  see also ethnographic research;
    qualitative research;
    quantifying method;
    quantitative research;
    sociology
social structure, of modern society,
  105–7
society, emerging concept of,
  10–11, 22–3
sociological imagination, 7
Sociological Imagination, The, 86
sociology
  classical period of, 39
  influence of, 158–61
  as literature genre, 161–5
solutions, and deduction, 31–2
stake inoculation, 149, 151
statistical research
  Durkheim's work, 44–5, 47–8, 55
  growth of, 19
  interviews and observations,
    48–52
  official statistics, 11–12
  see also quantifying method
stories
  analysis of, 116–17, 118–20
  audience reception of, 122–4
  life-stories, 126–7
  schema theory of interpretation,
    125–6, 127
  see also Western films
Street Corner Society, 111

structuralism
  approach to narratives *see*
    narrative structure
  and concept of homology,
    108–11
  contribution to social research,
    103, 112
  emergence of, 99
  features of, 112–13
  influence on Durkheim, 103–5
  Saussure's theory of language,
    99–102
  structure of modern society,
    106–7
  use of term, 98
structure, ontological status of, 113
structures of expectation, 150
Suicide, 44–5, 47–8
Sulkunen, Pekka, 117–18
surveillance, 12–16
surveys
  limits and possibilities of, 53–7
  nature of, 135–41
  in quantitative approach, 49–52
  reliability and validity of,
    138–41
Sutcliffe, Claud, 54
symbolic interactionism, 99, 101
Symons, Julian, 83
syntagmatic analysis, 118–20

Tannen, Deborah, 150
television, audience reception of,
  123–4
theoretical frameworks
  in ethnography, 65–6, 70–1
  and methods adopted, 28–31,
    37–8, 129–30
  nature of, 164
  for survey analyses, 57
therapeutic interviews, 145
Thompson, E.P., 163
Thrasher, Frederick, 73
totemism, 104–5
Touraine, Alain, 89–90, 91–2
*Treatise of Taxes and Contributions,
  A*, 11, 17–18

urban society
  literature genres in, 20–1
  surveillance in, 15–16

validity
  of ethnography, 62–3
  of in-depth interviews, 144–5
  of survey data, 139–41
variables
  in experimental design, 46, 47–8
  in surveys, 53–4
Vilkko, Anni, 126–7

Way Some People Die, The, 133

Weber, Max, 79
Western films, analysis of, 120–2
Wetherell, Margaret, 127
White, Hayden, 163
Whyte, William Foote, 74, 111
Widdicombe, Sue, 149
Willis, Paul, 68, 109–10
women's studies, 161
Wooffitt, Robin, 149
working class, studies of, 72–3,
    106–7, 109–10
Wright, Will, 120–2

youth cultures, studies of, 70,
    73–5, 109, 111, 149, 151